Lightning Licks

Presents

The No Need to Read Series

Guitar Chord Bible

Content created by Rockero Media LLC
www.rockeromedia.com
This book Copyright © 2011 by
Rockero Media LLC Publications
International Copyright Secured. All Rights Reserved.

Lightning Licks is a Division of Rockero Media.
Visit Lightning Licks at www.LightningLicks.com.

No part of this publication may be reproduced in any form or by any means without the prior written permission of the Publisher.

Mayuli Press

© 2013 Mayuli Press
http://mayuli.com/
Made in USA
All Rights Reserved
ISBN: 978-0-9857549-3-8

Table of Contents

How to Read the Chord Diagrams	4
C chords	5-12
D chords	13-16
E chords	17-24
F chords	25-32
G chords	33-40
A chords	41-44
B chords	45-52

How to Read the Chord Diagrams

Fretboxes show the guitar upright i.e. with the headstock, nut and tuning pegs at the top of the picture. Six vertical lines represent the strings.

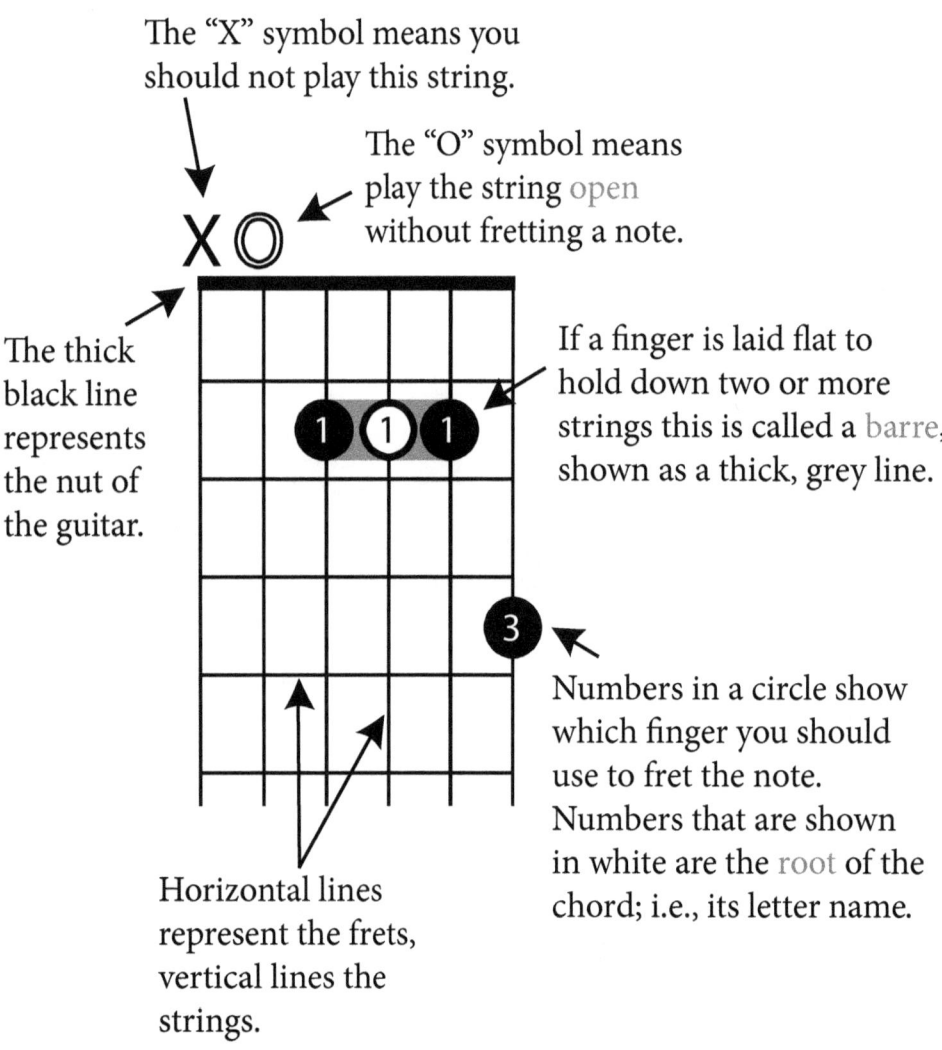

The "X" symbol means you should not play this string.

The "O" symbol means play the string open without fretting a note.

The thick black line represents the nut of the guitar.

If a finger is laid flat to hold down two or more strings this is called a barre, shown as a thick, grey line.

Numbers in a circle show which finger you should use to fret the note. Numbers that are shown in white are the root of the chord; i.e., its letter name.

Horizontal lines represent the frets, vertical lines the strings.

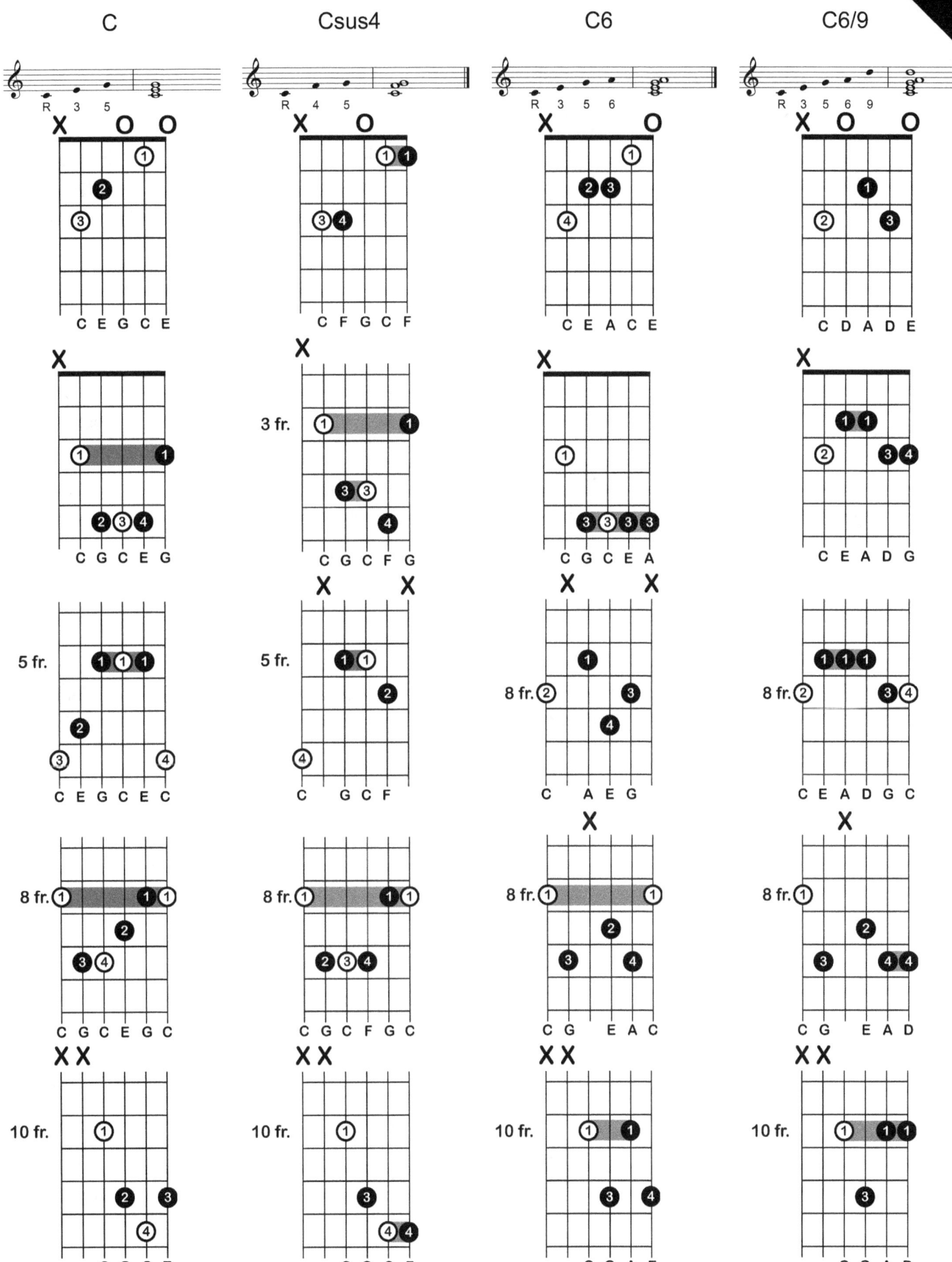

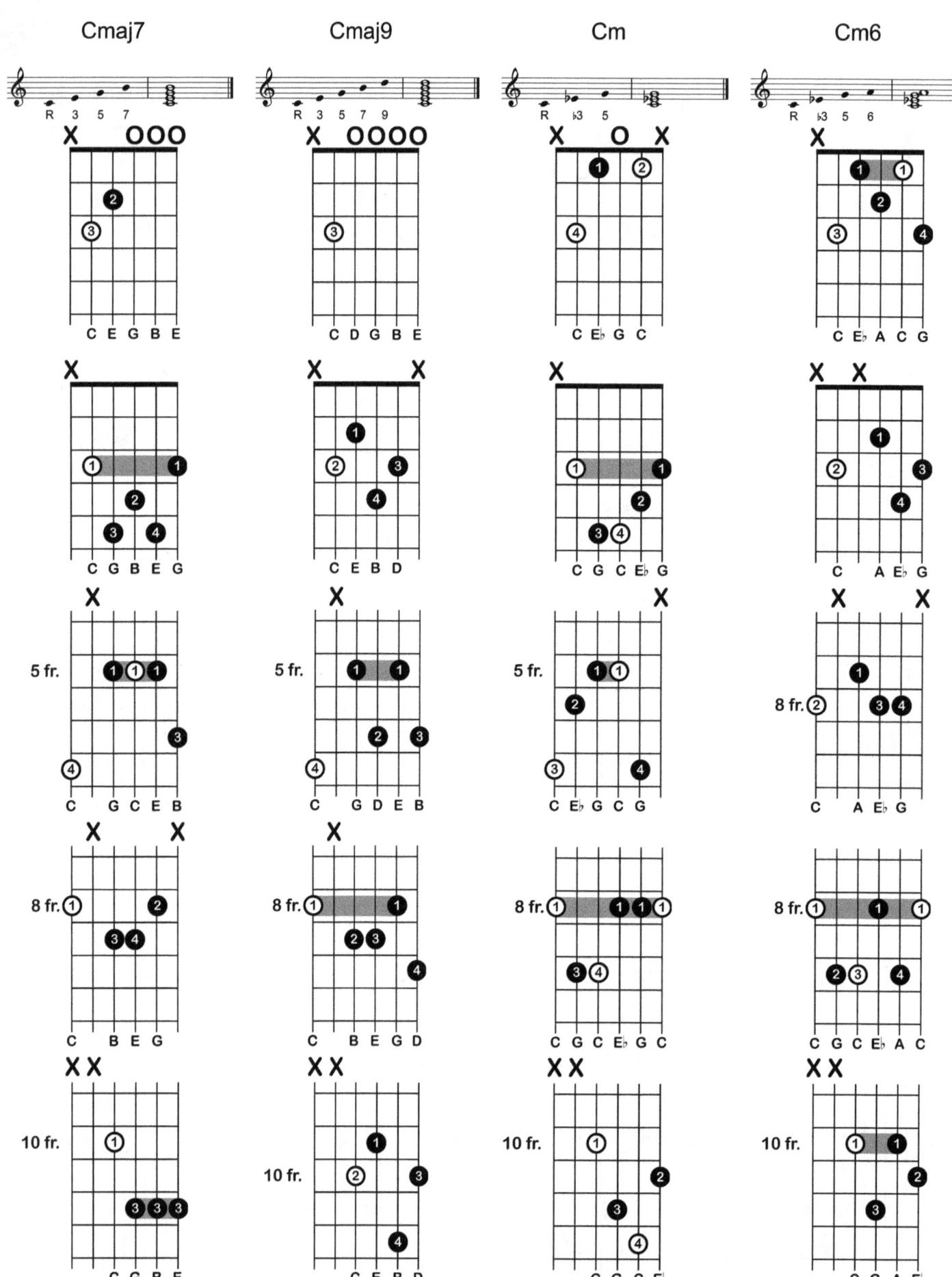

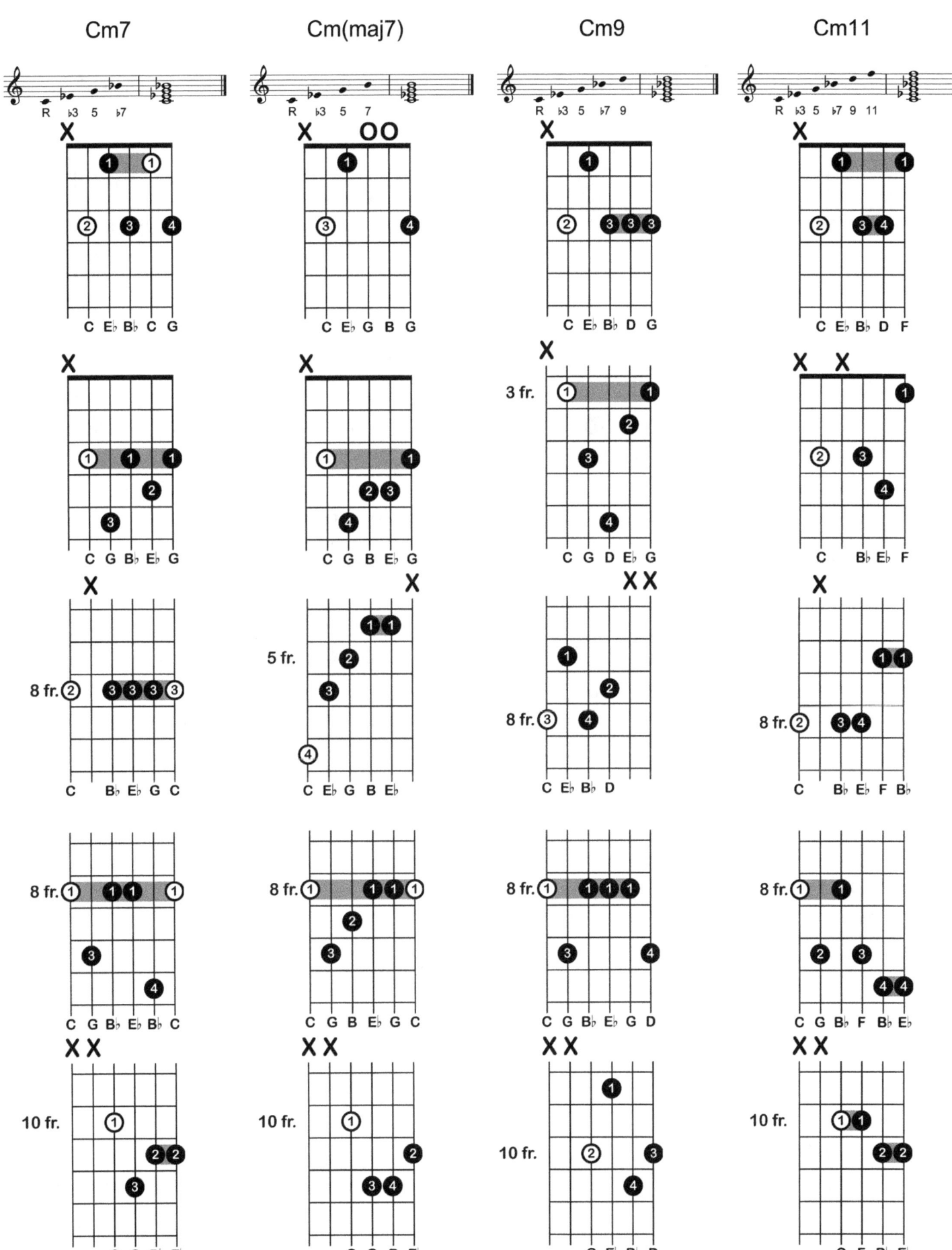

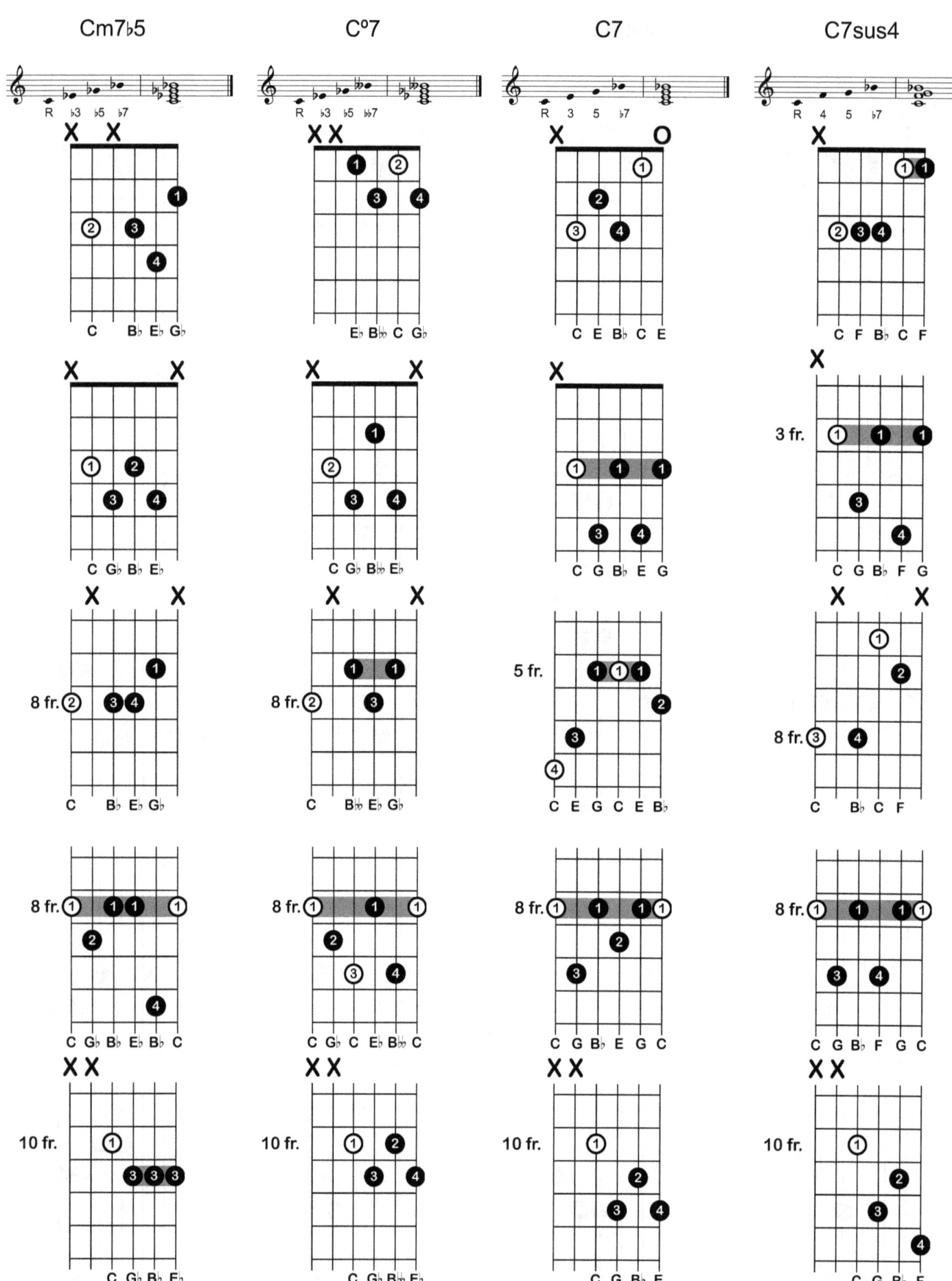

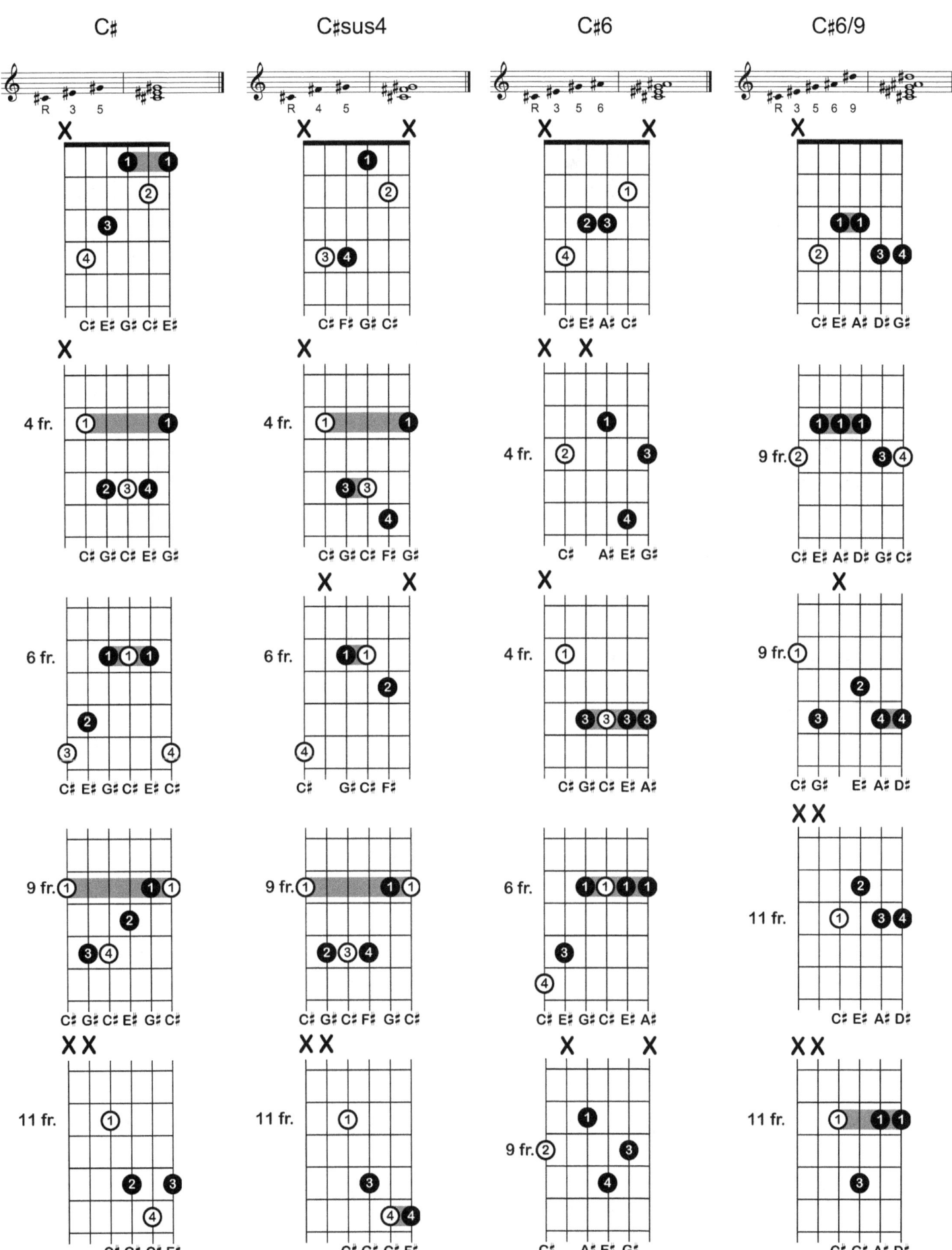

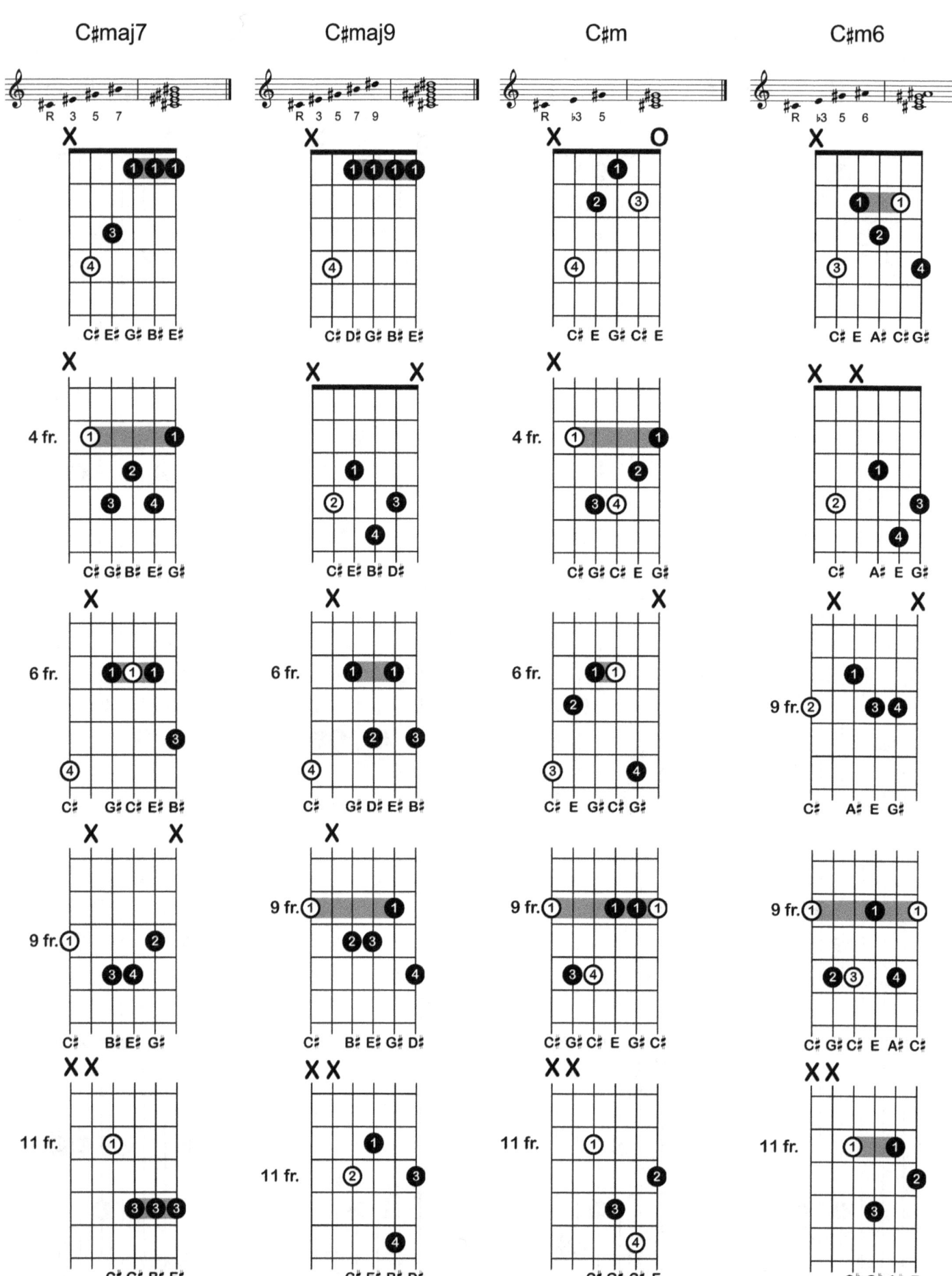

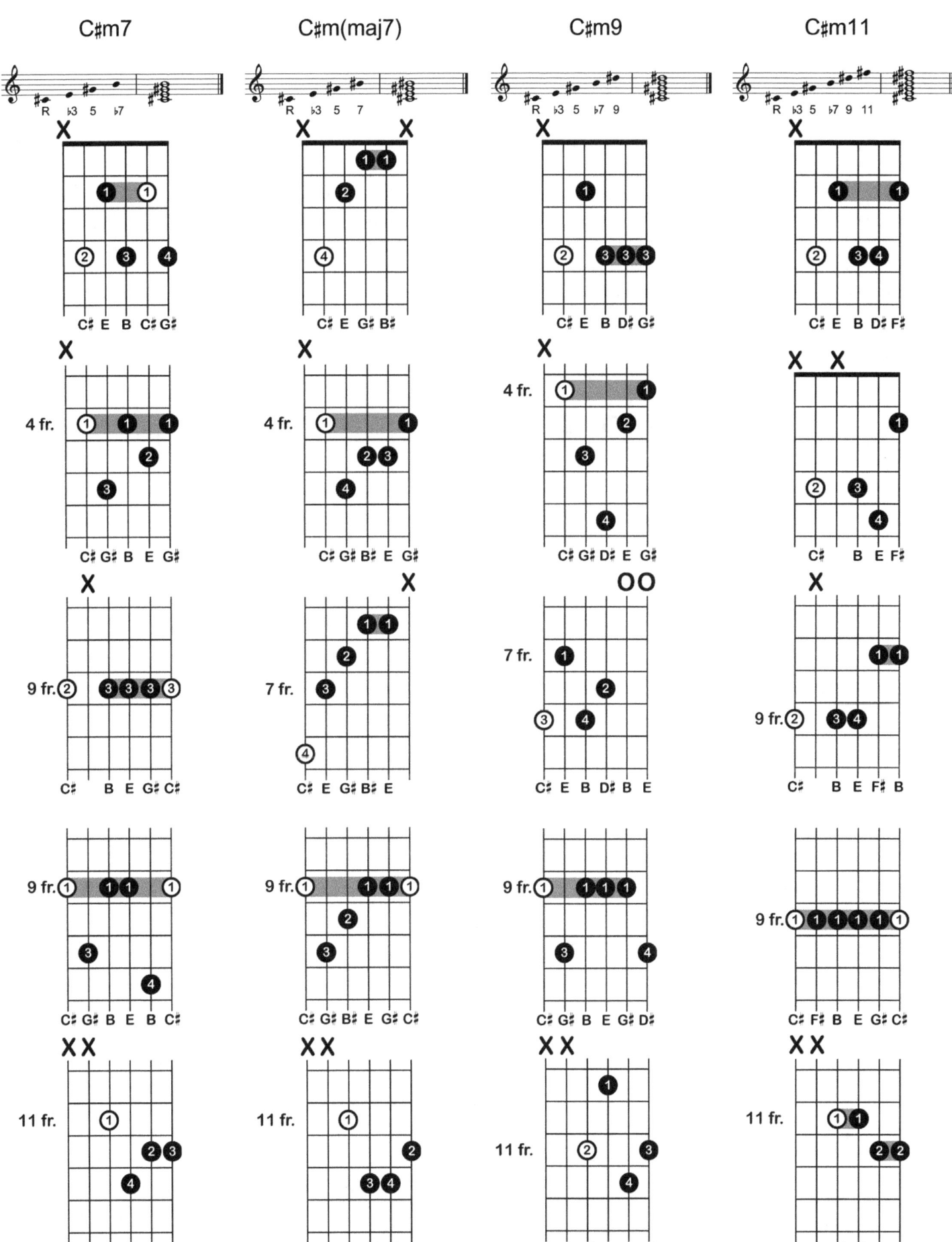

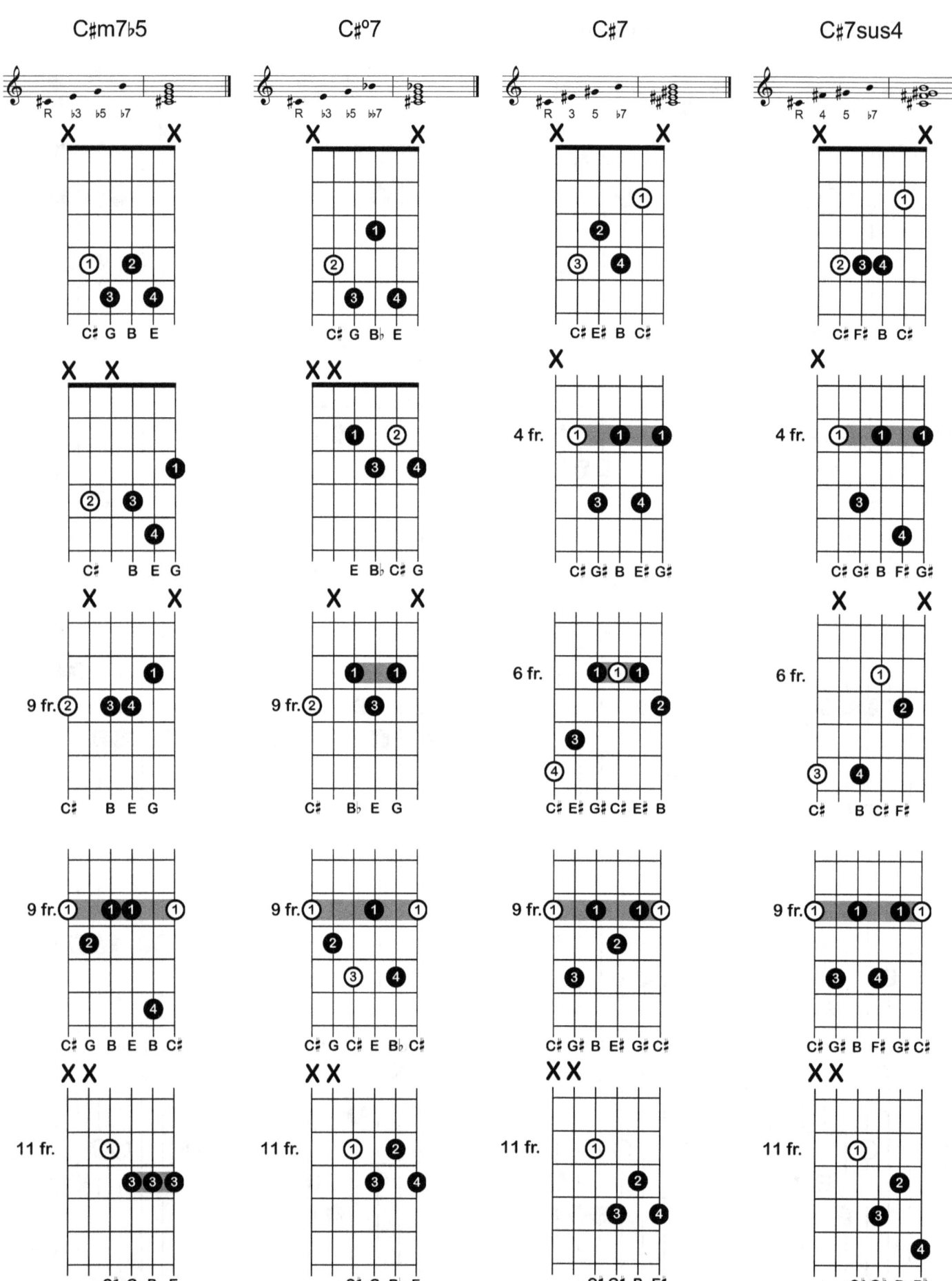

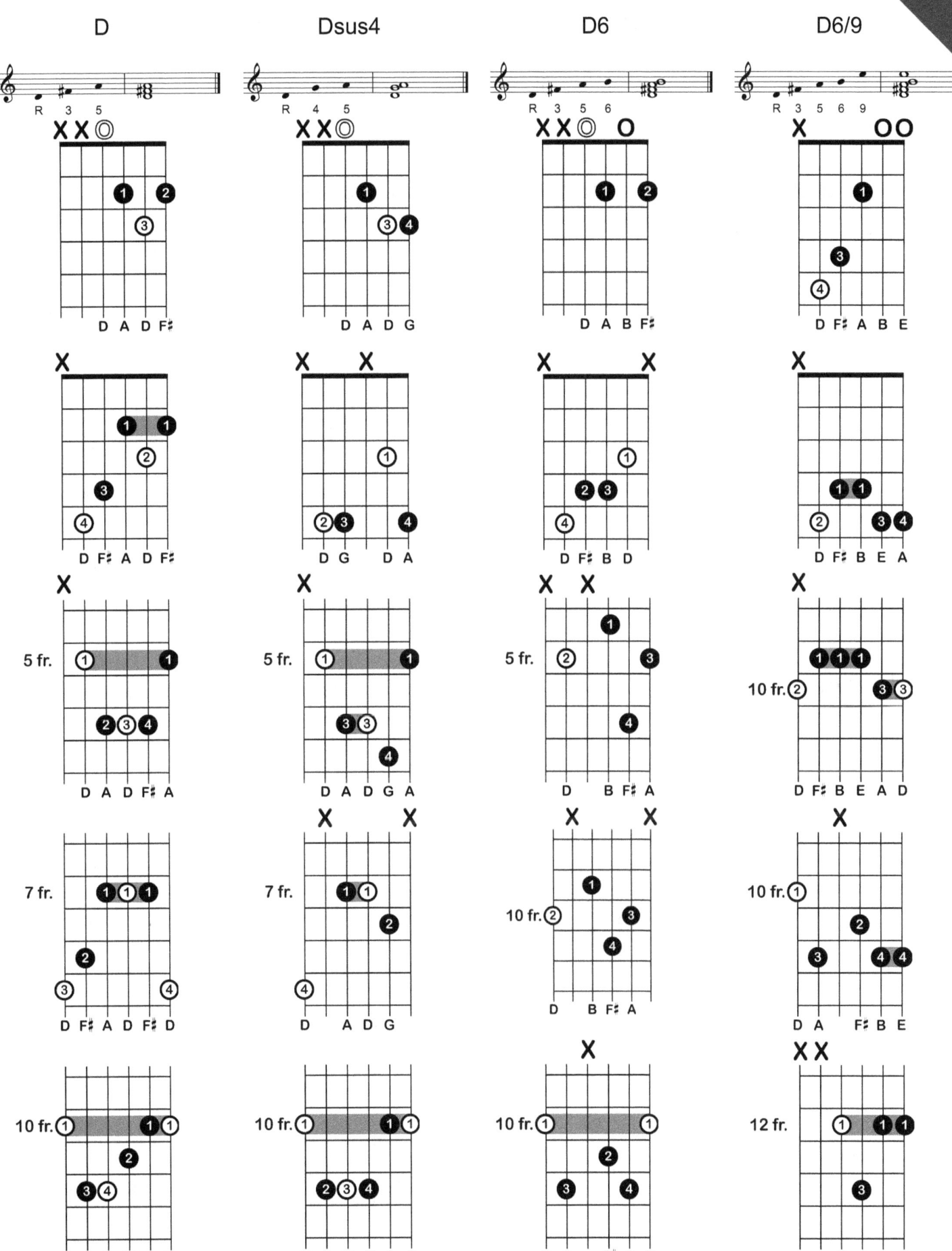

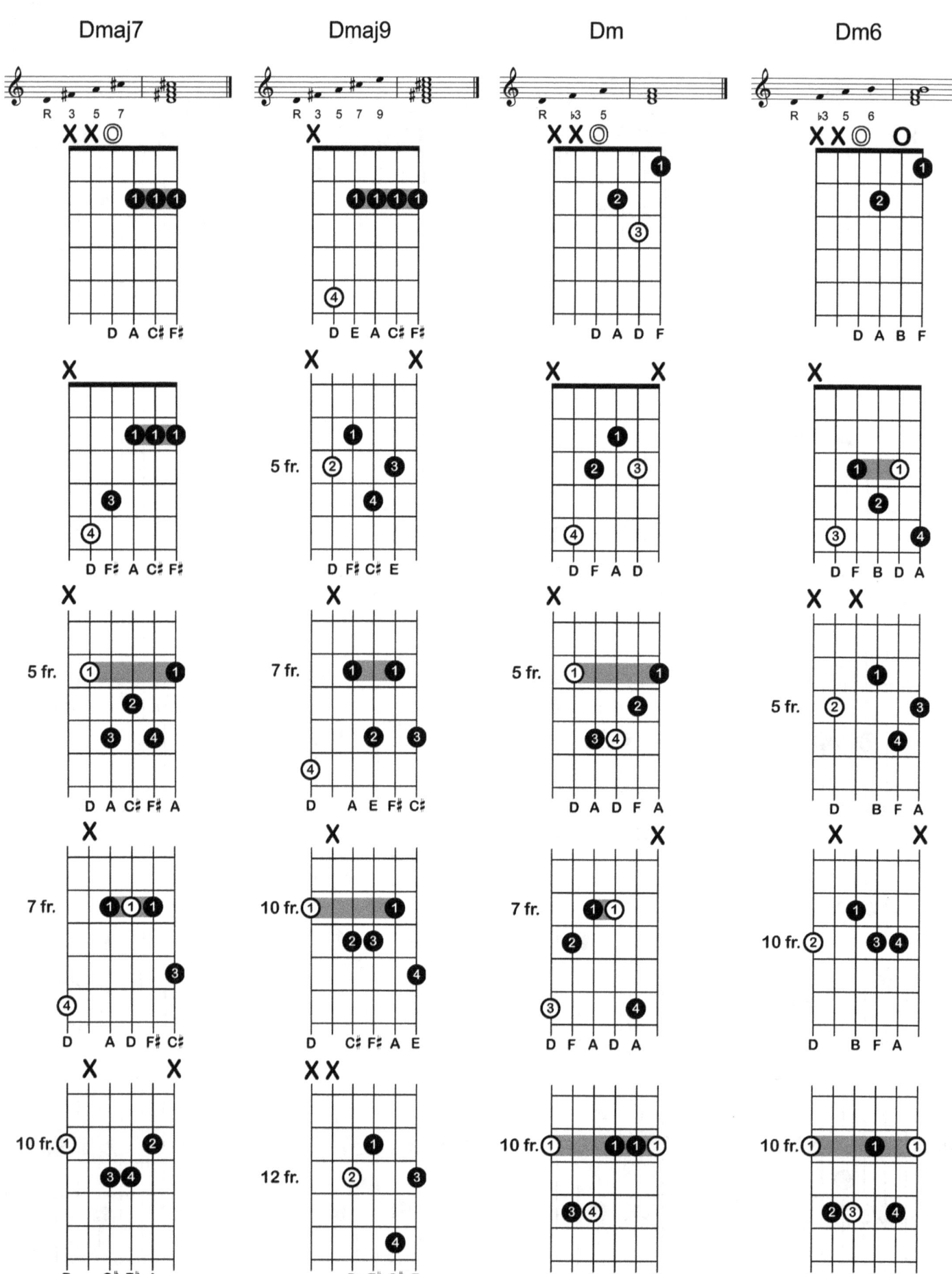

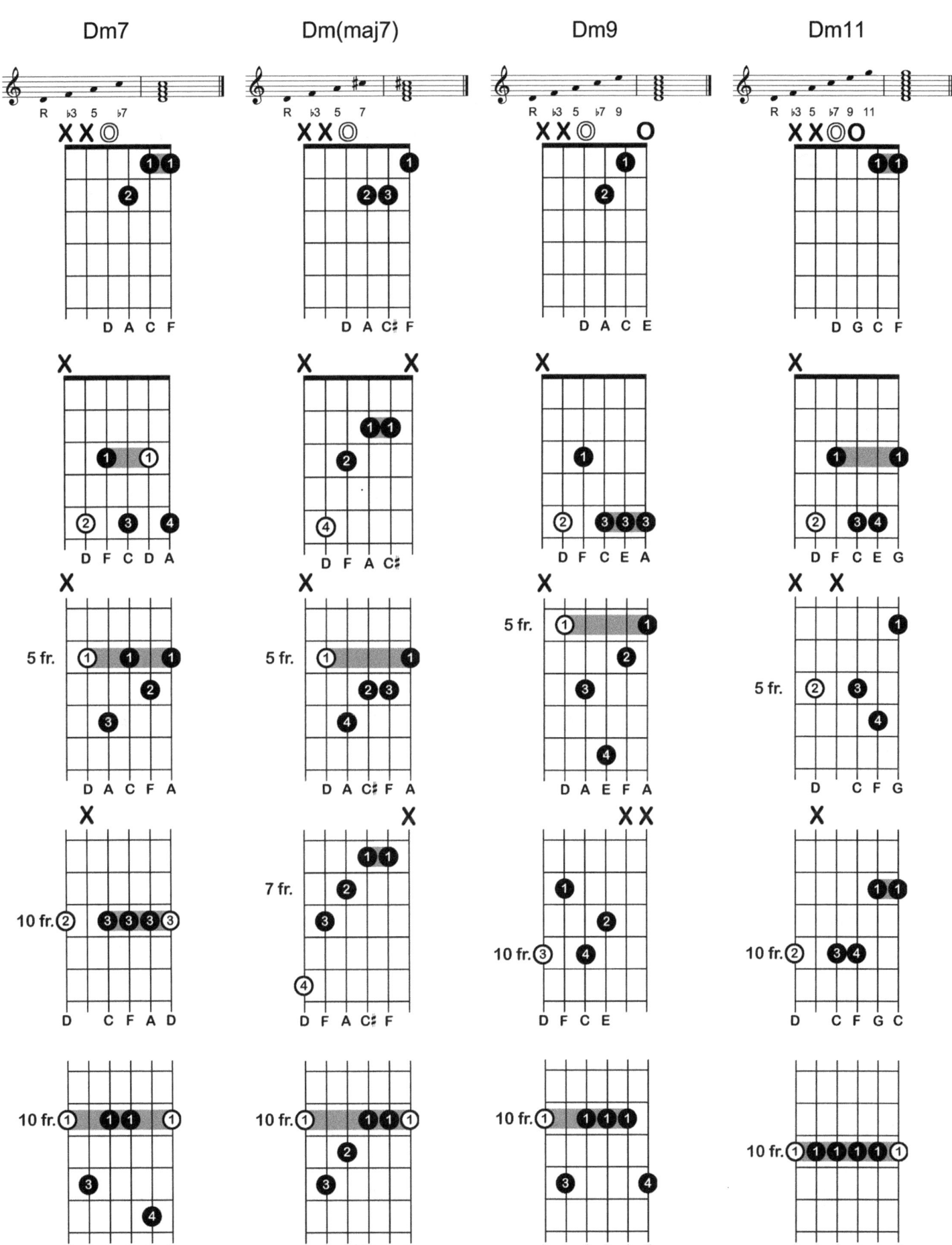

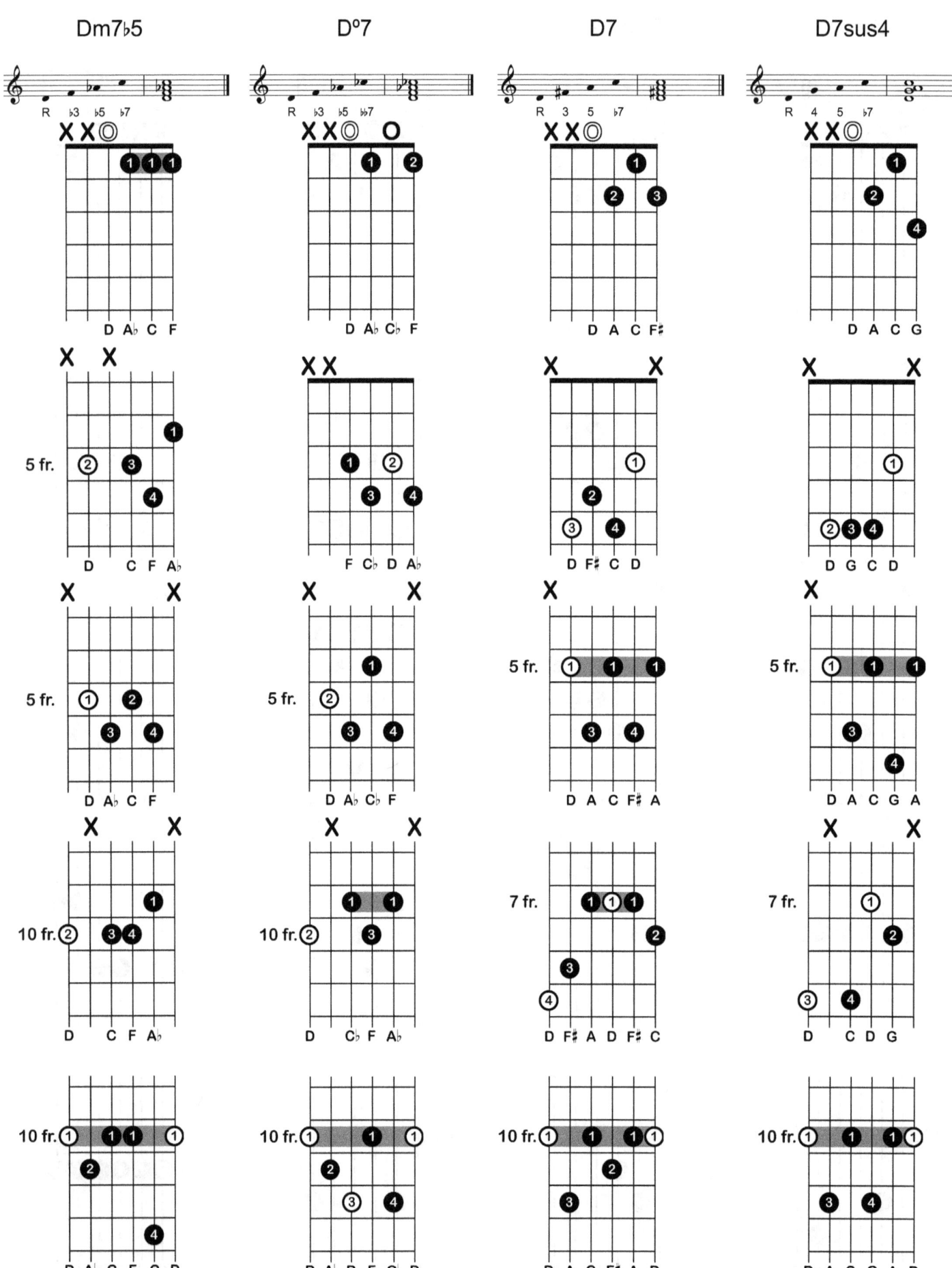

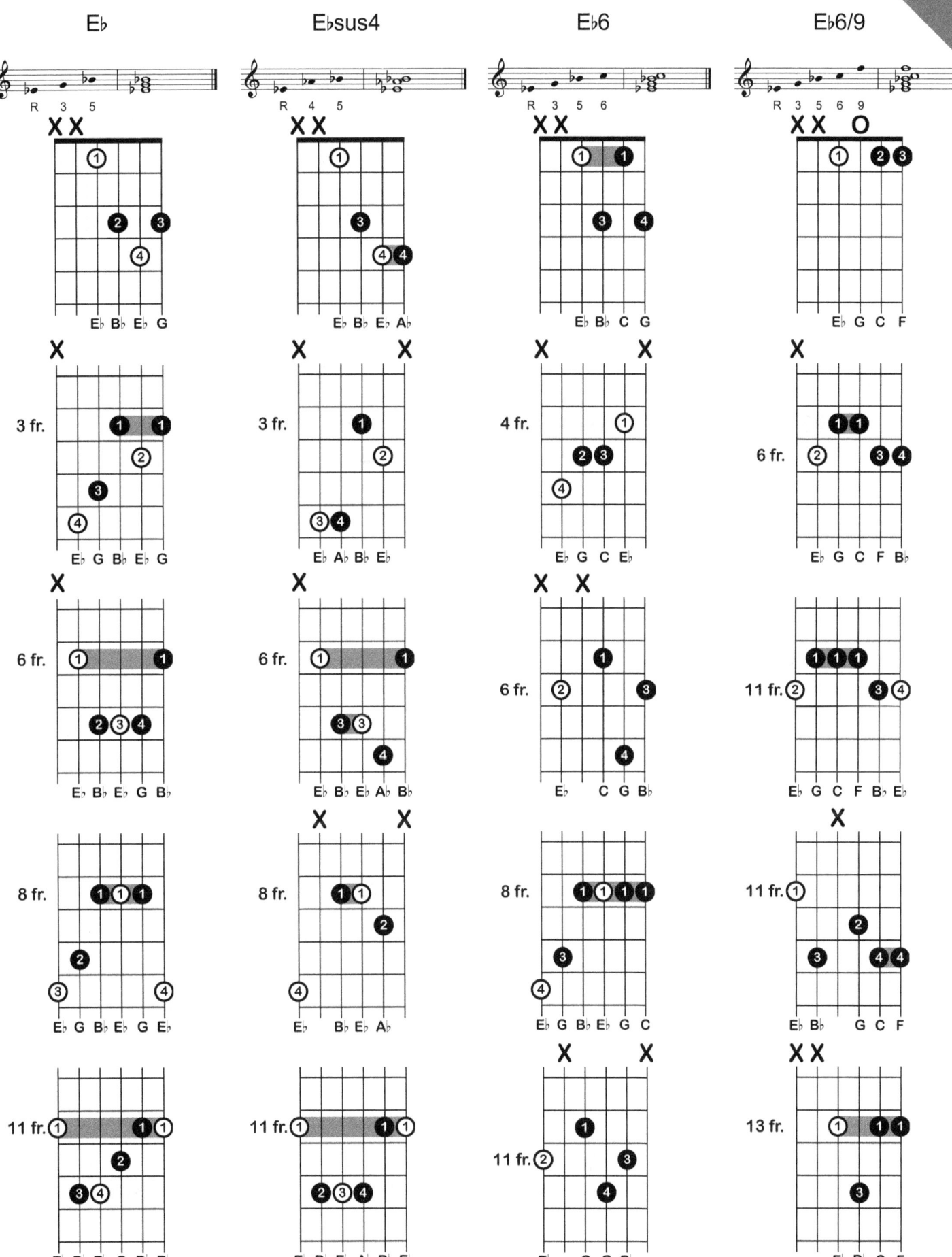

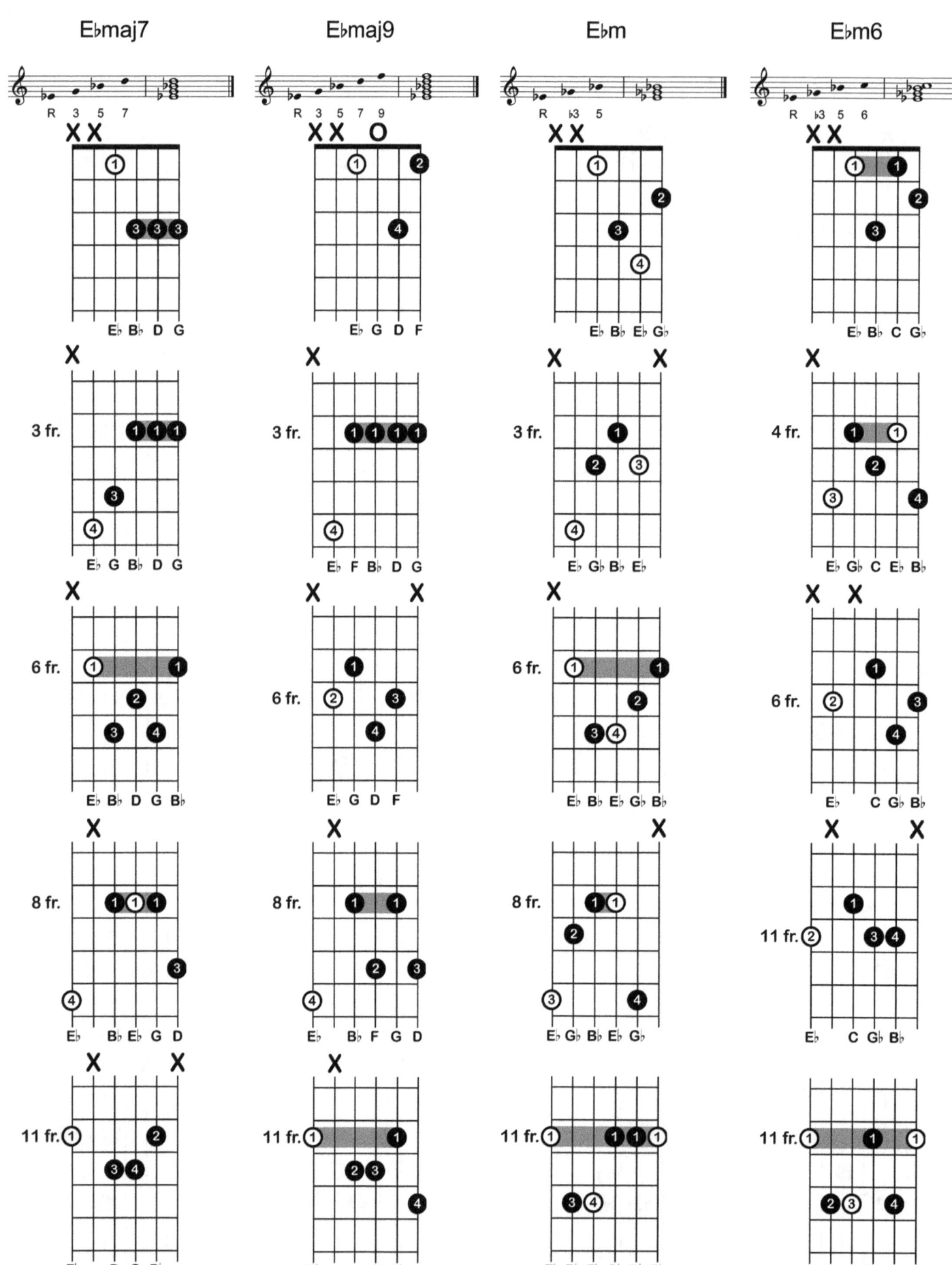

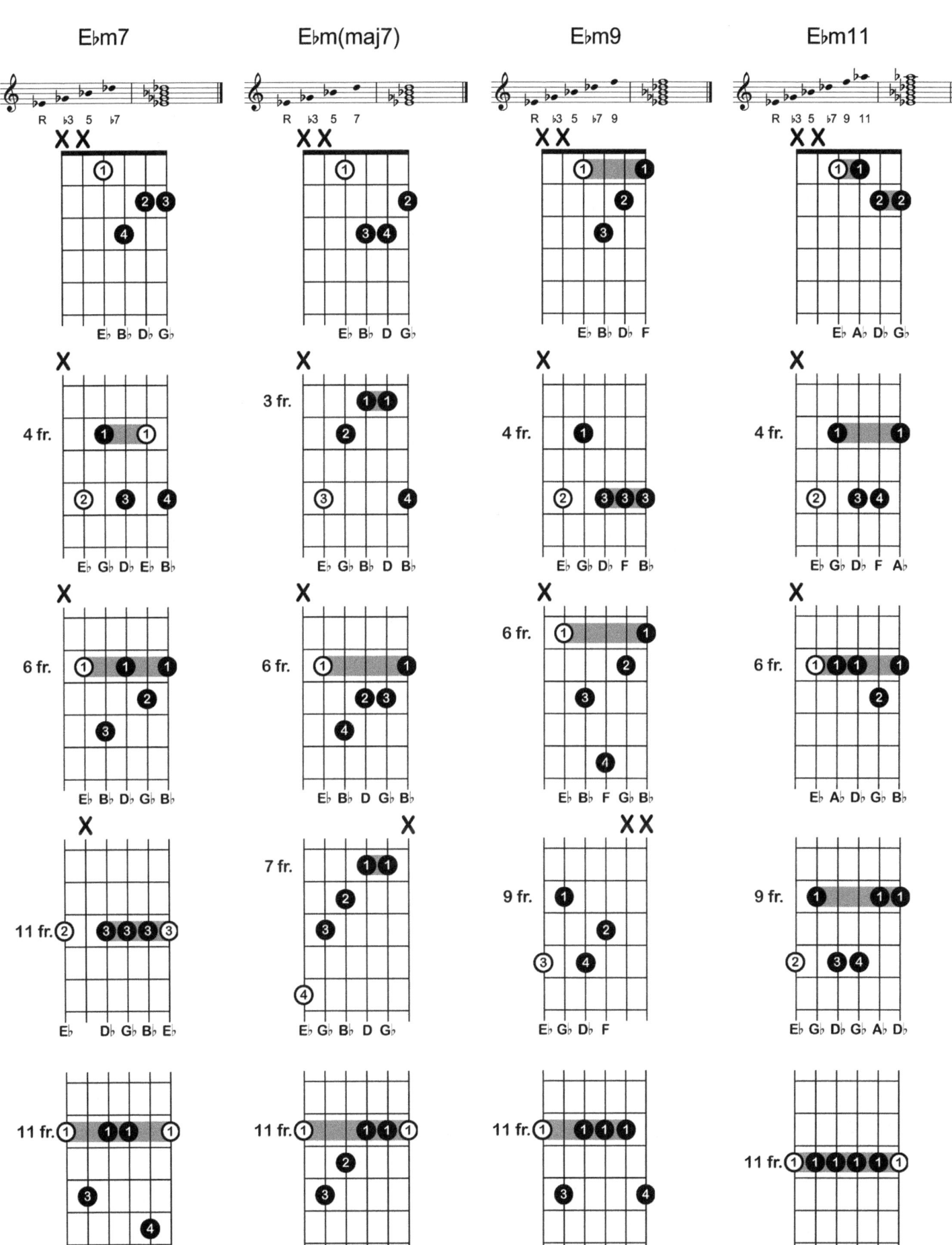

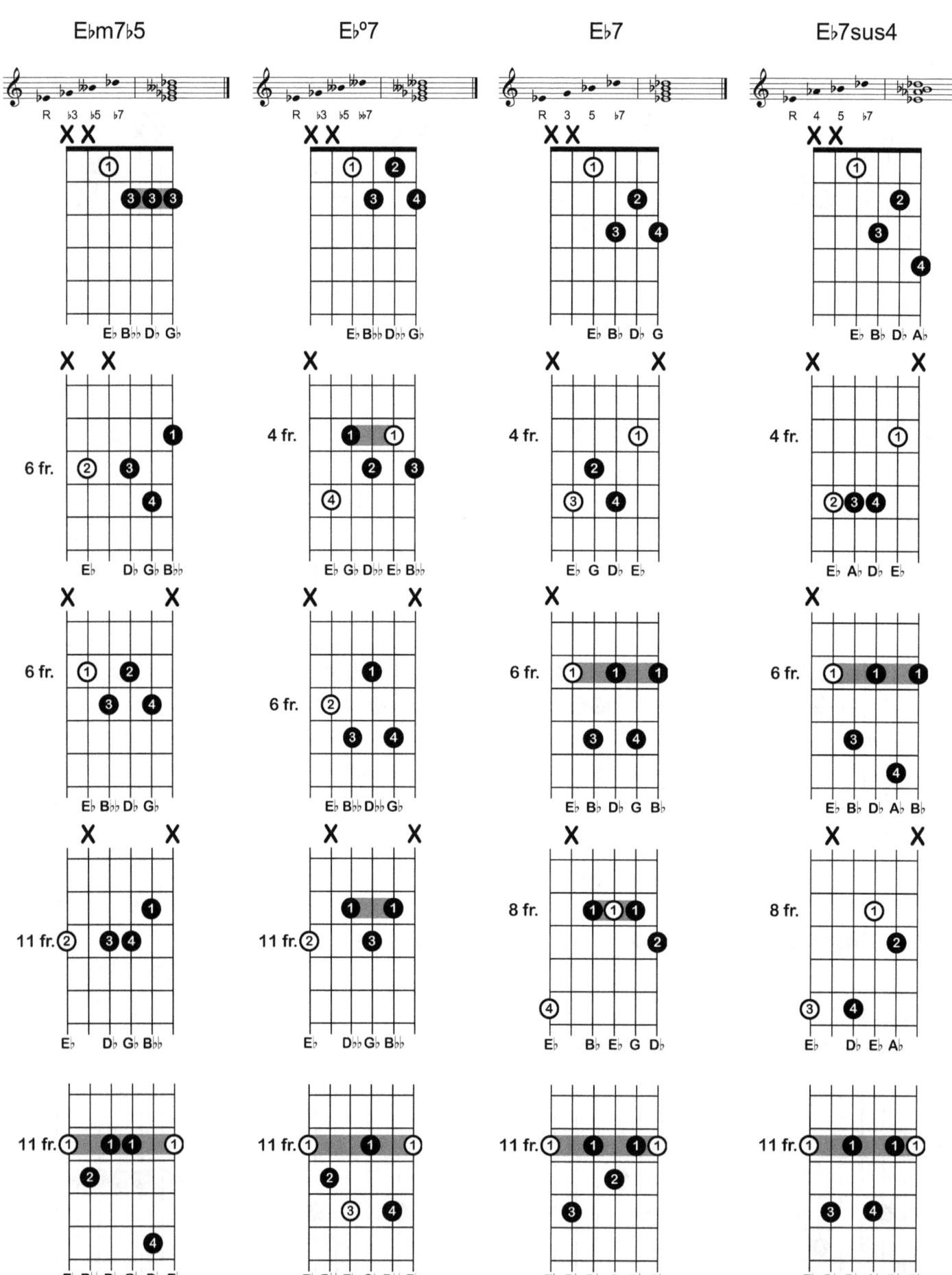

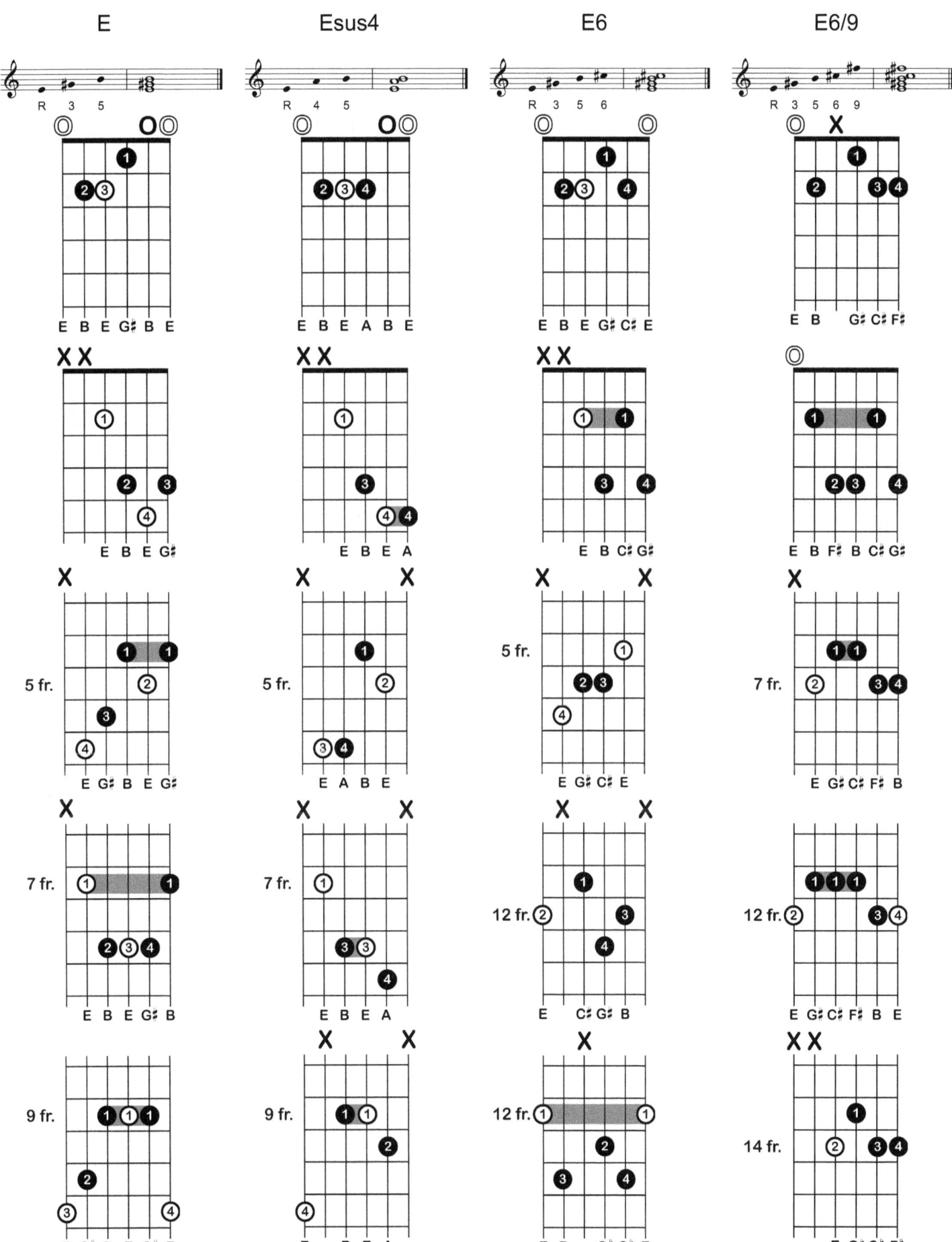

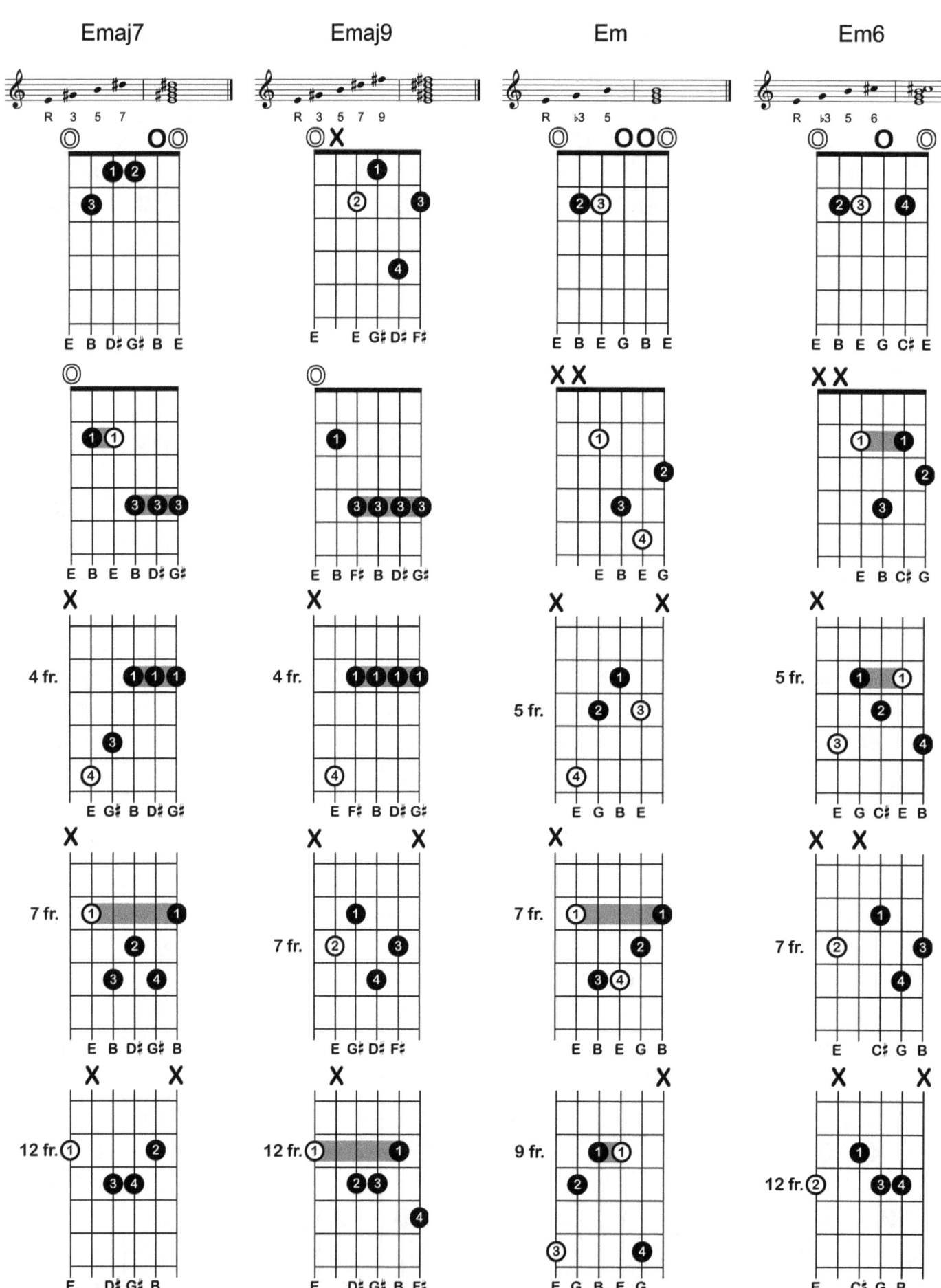

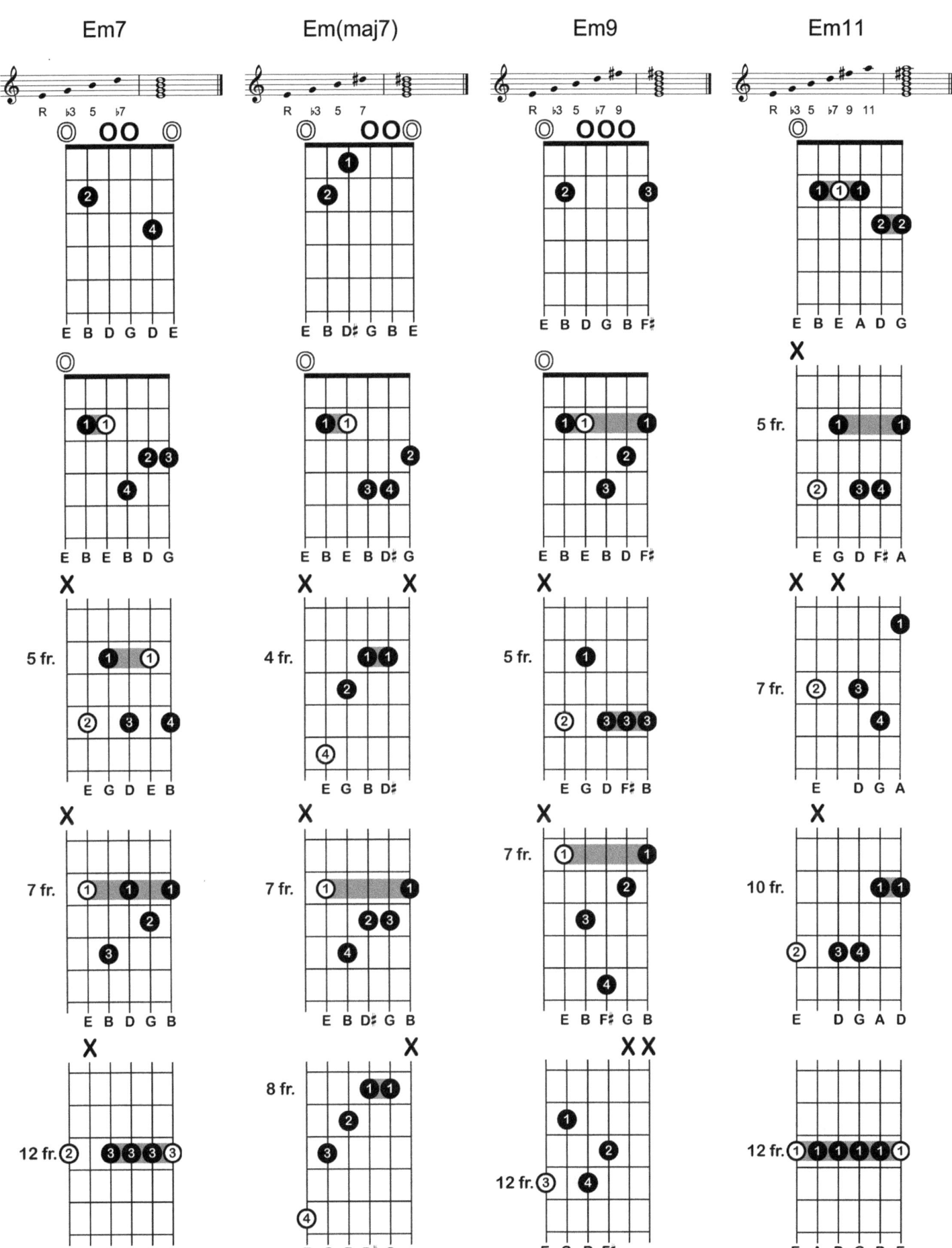

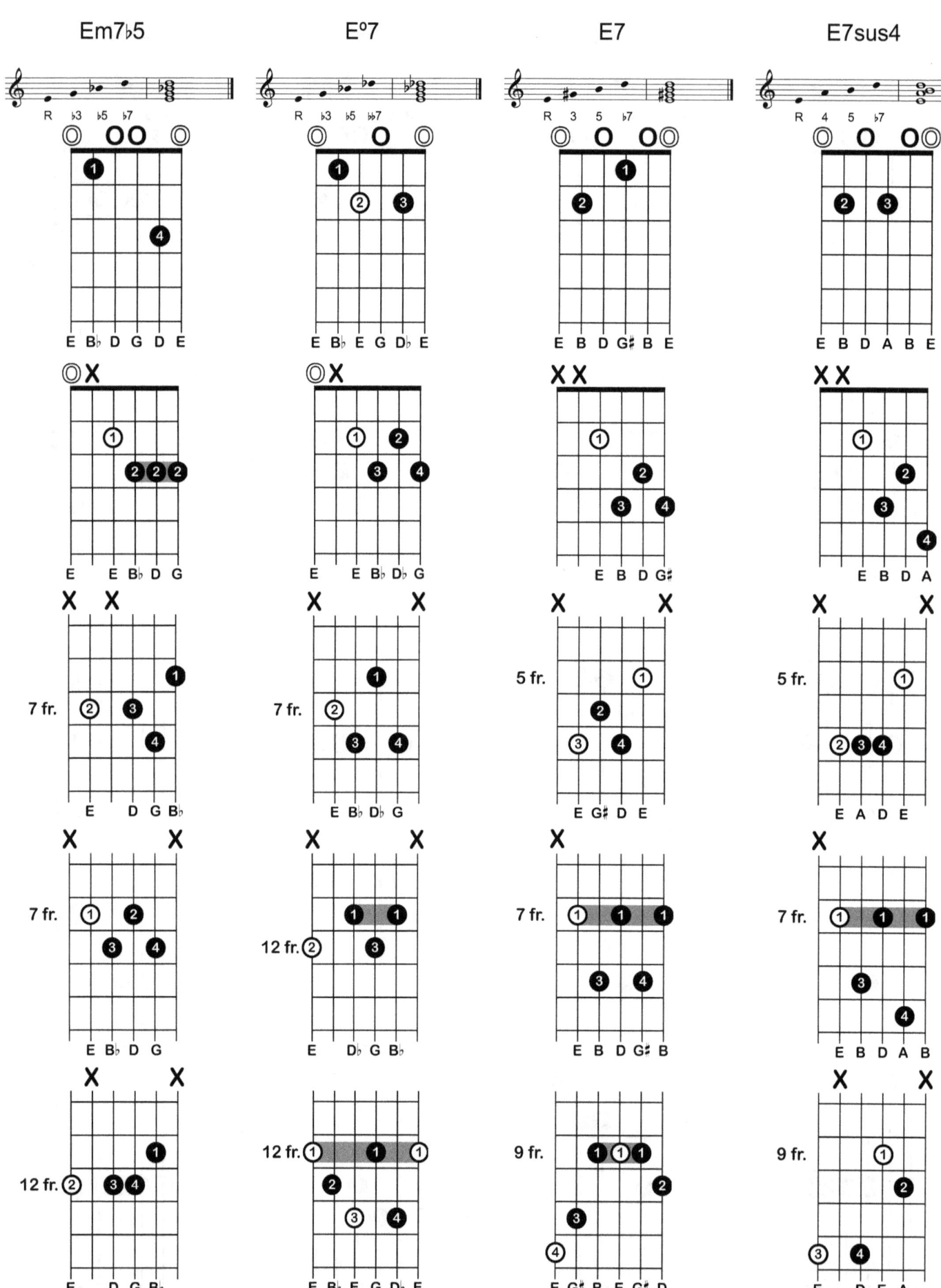

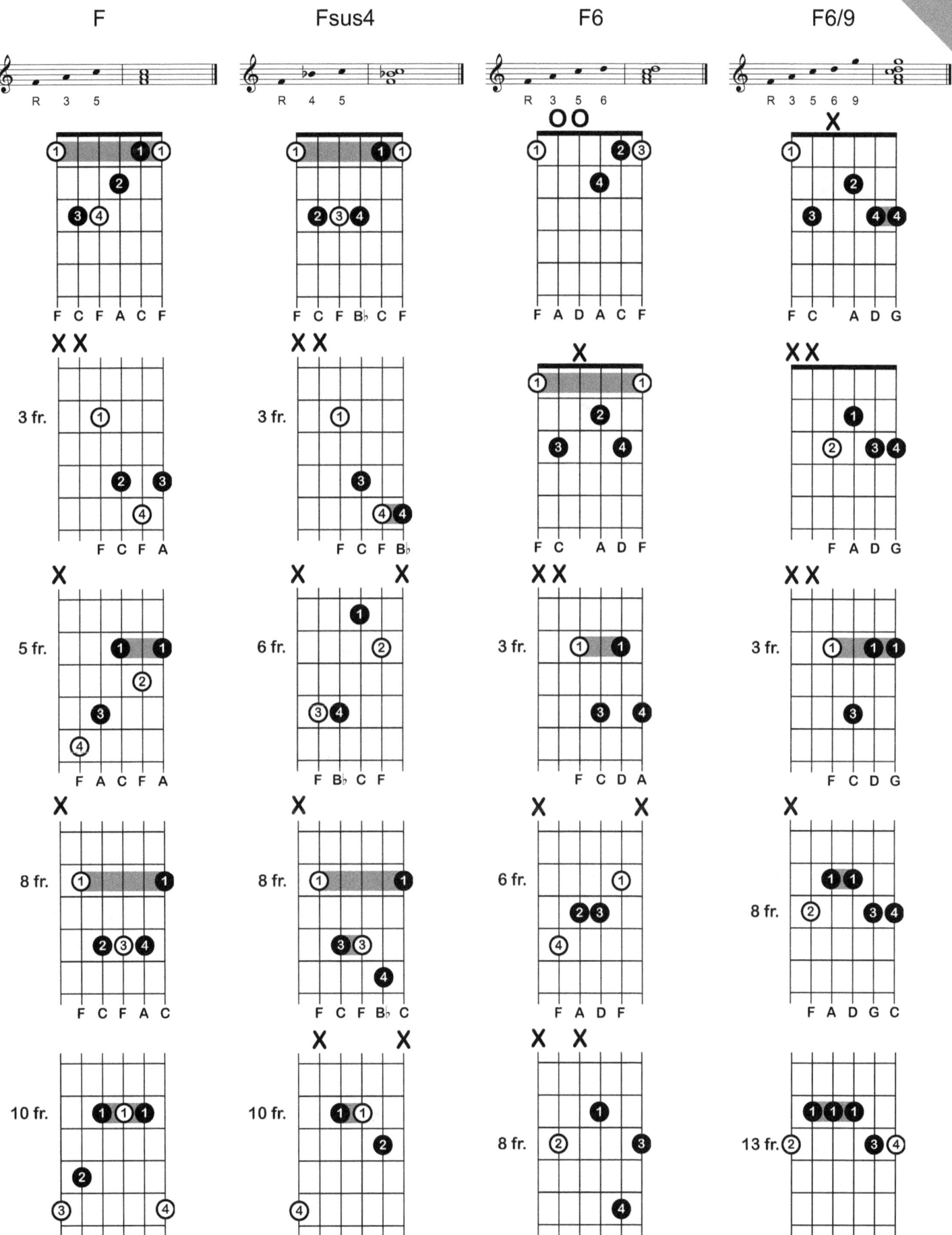

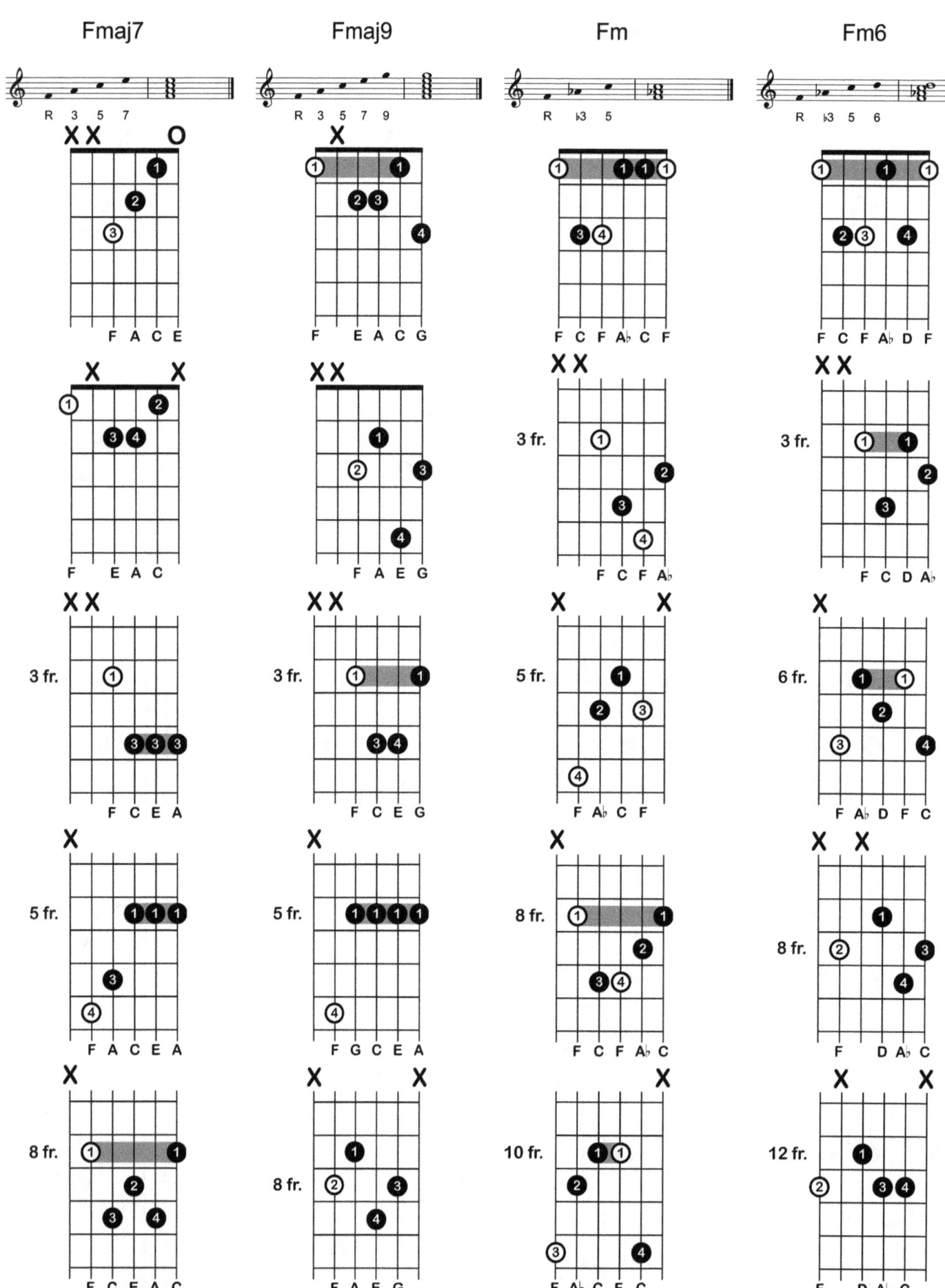

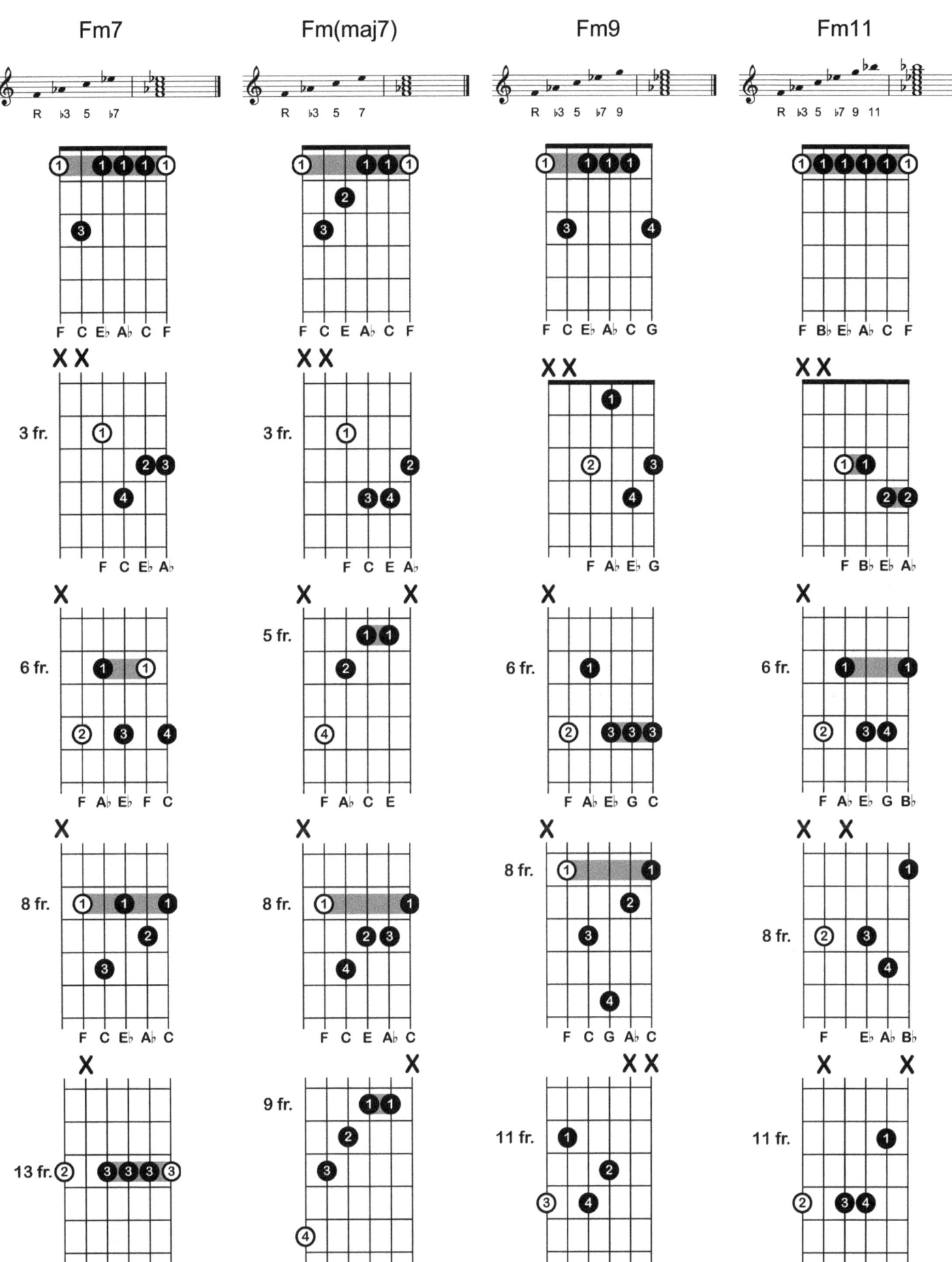

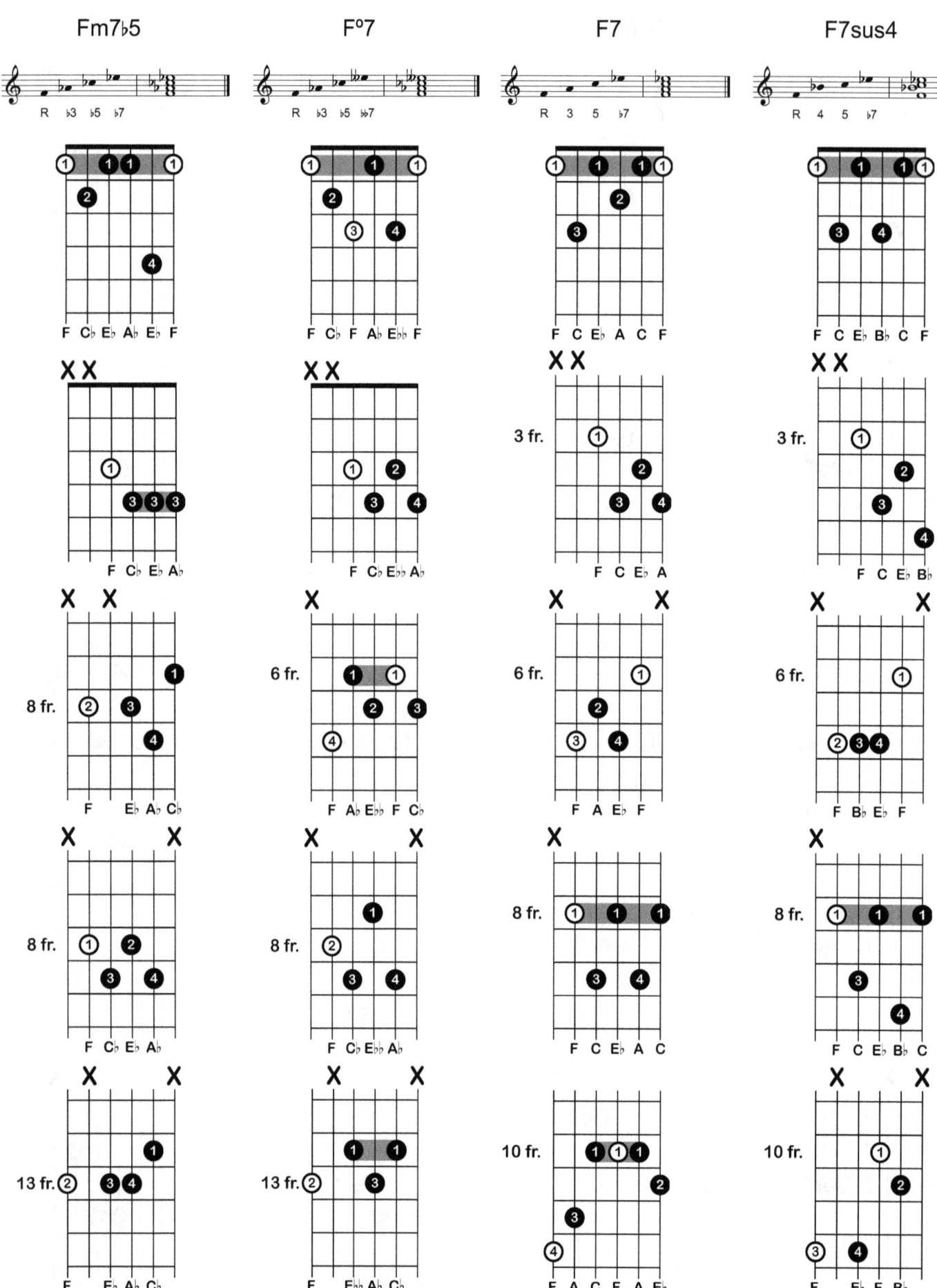

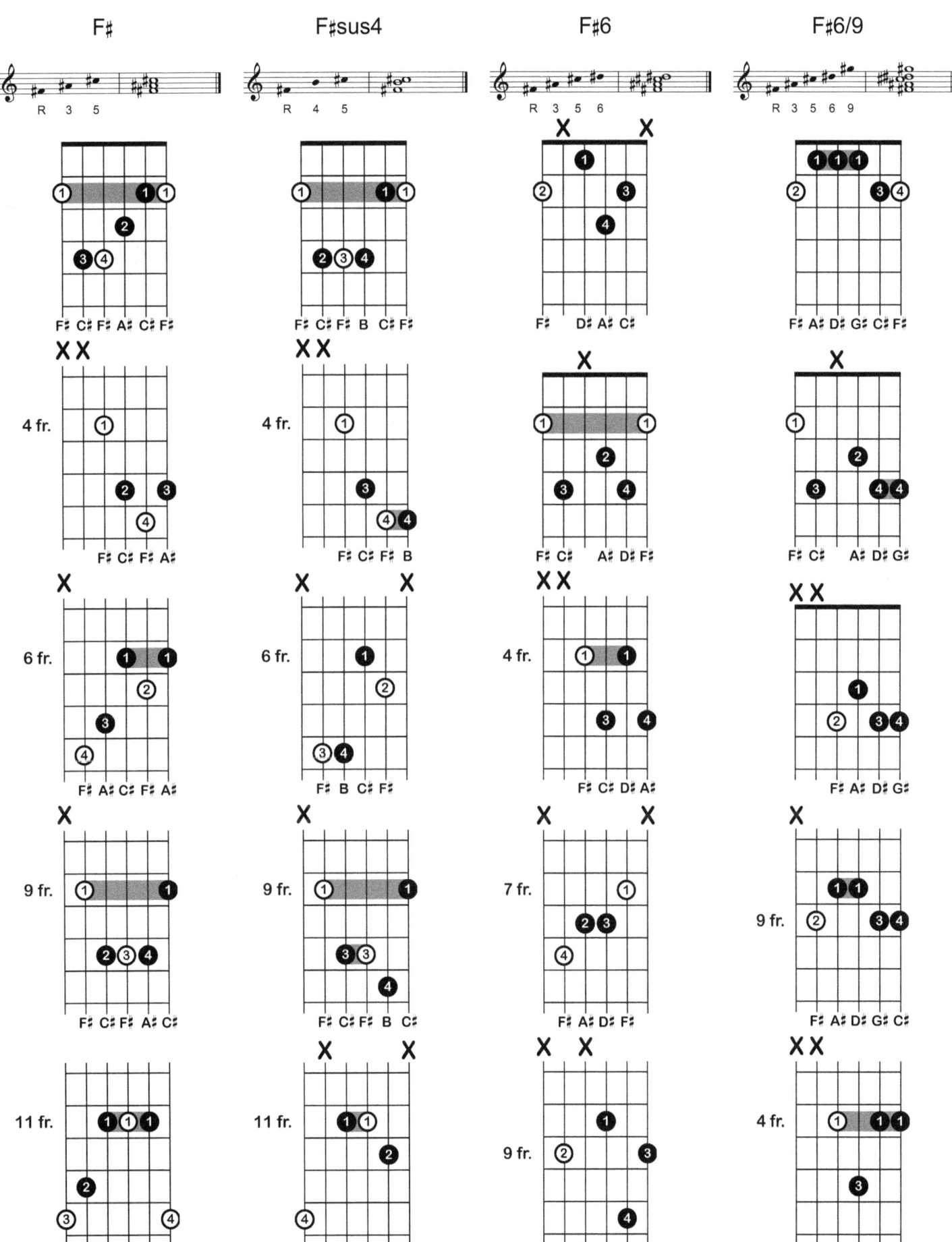

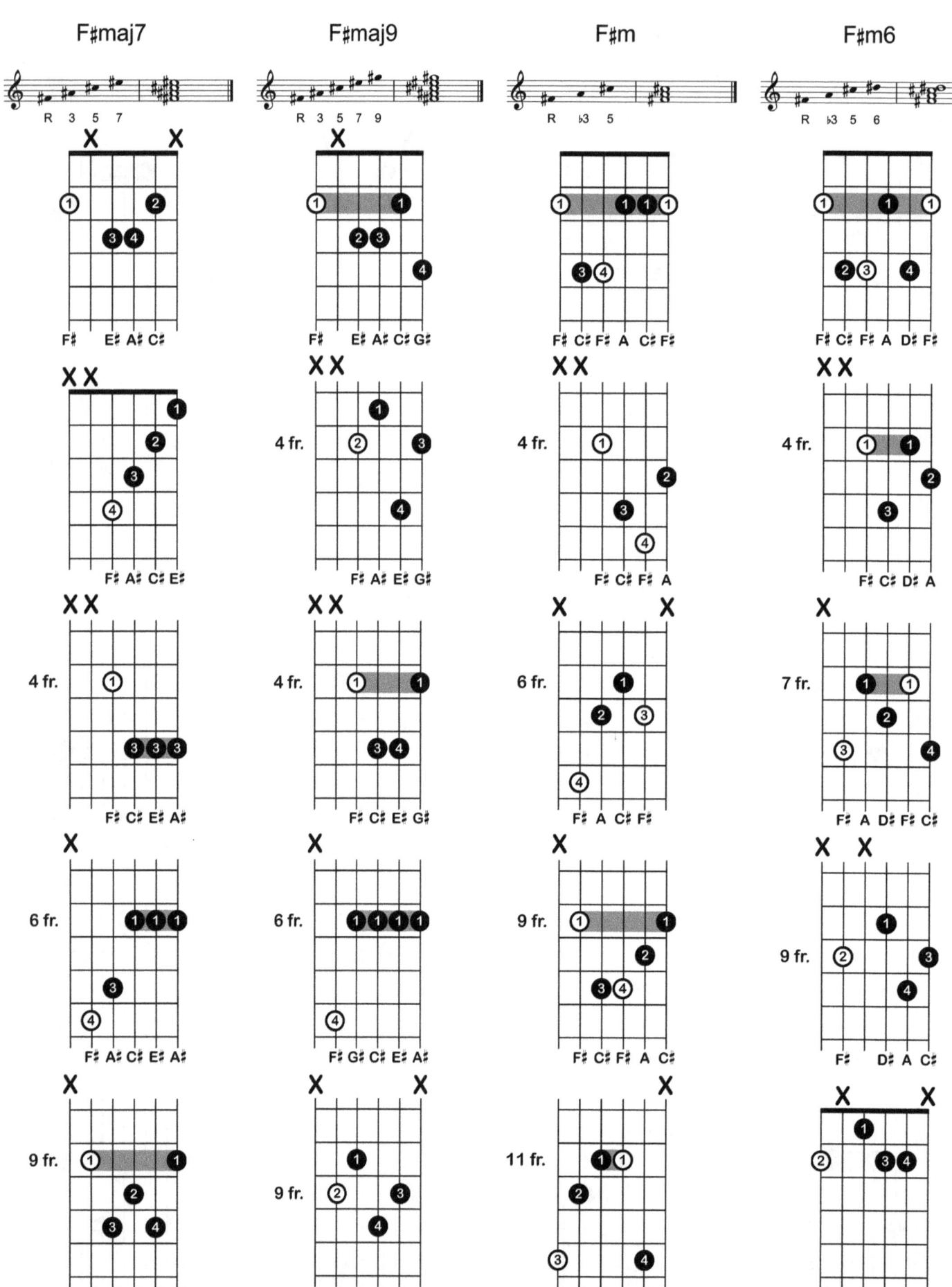

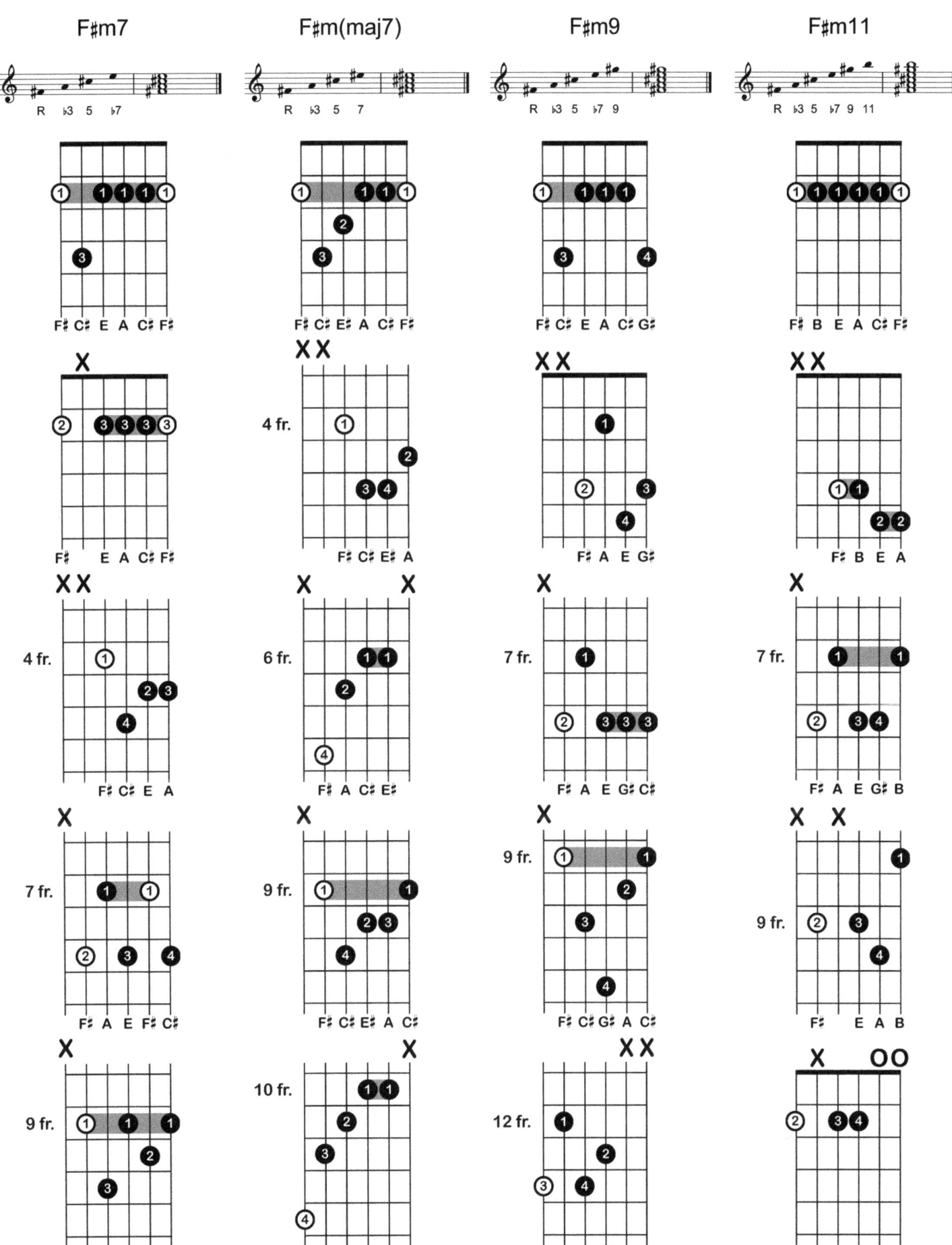

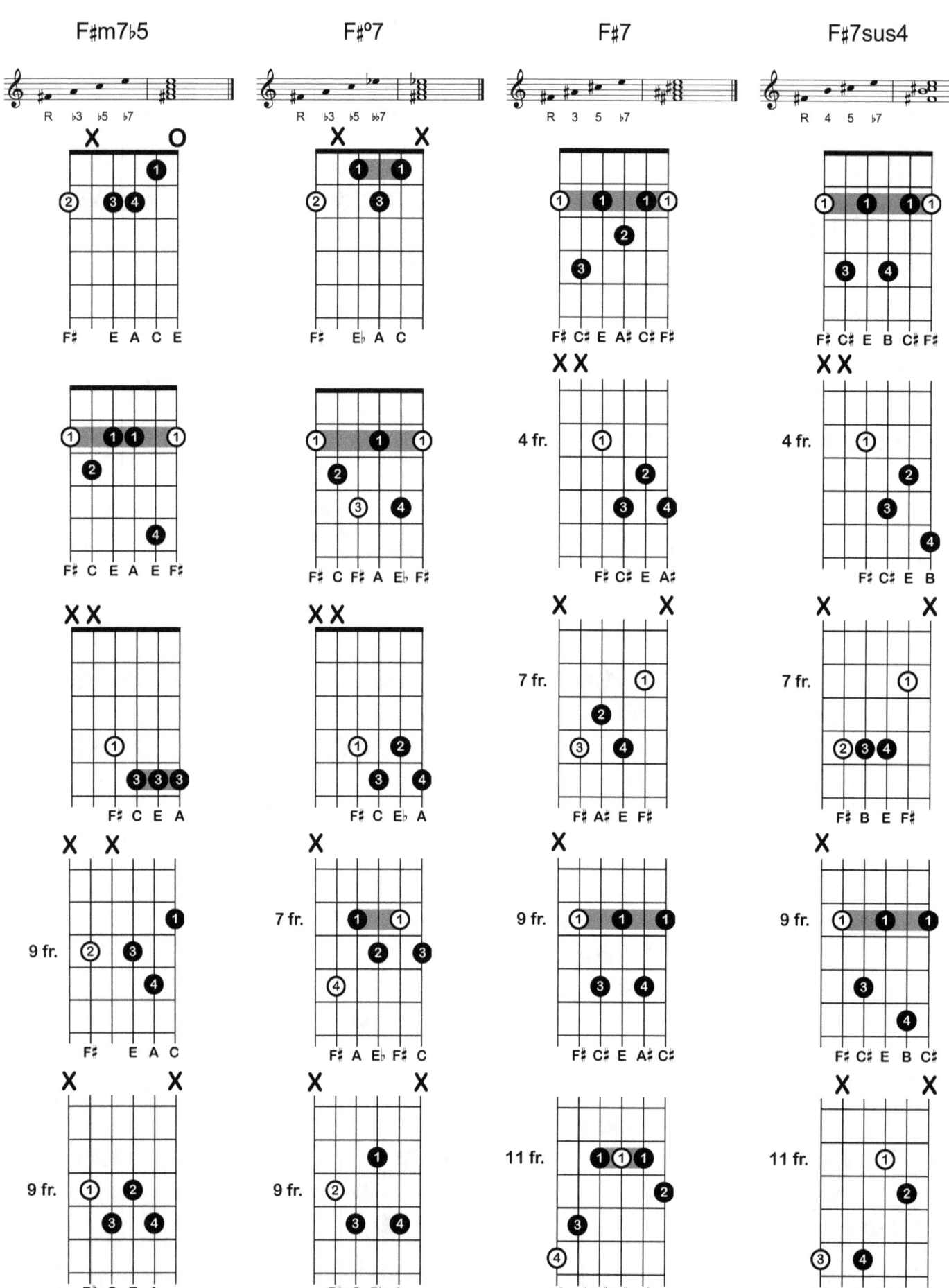

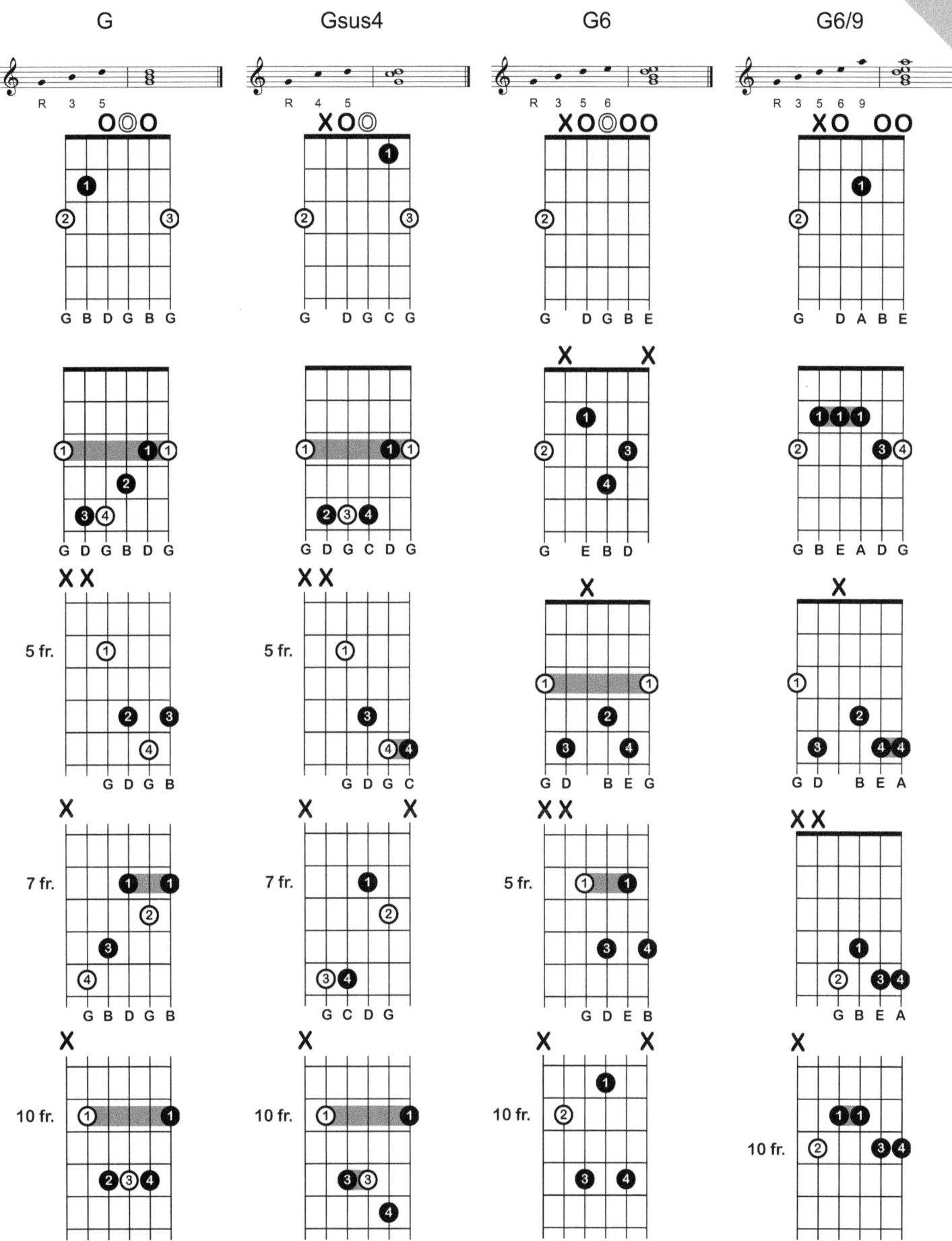

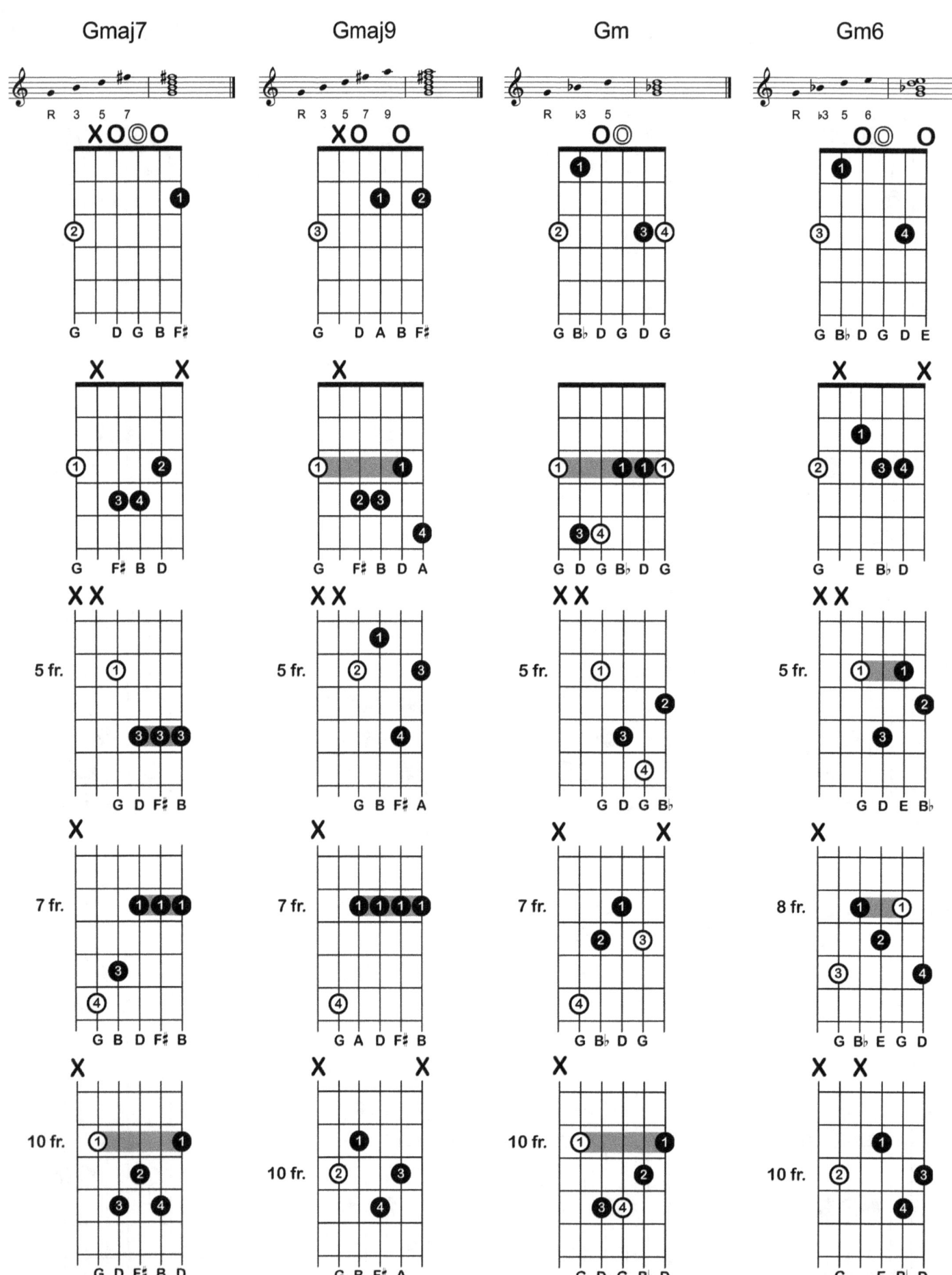

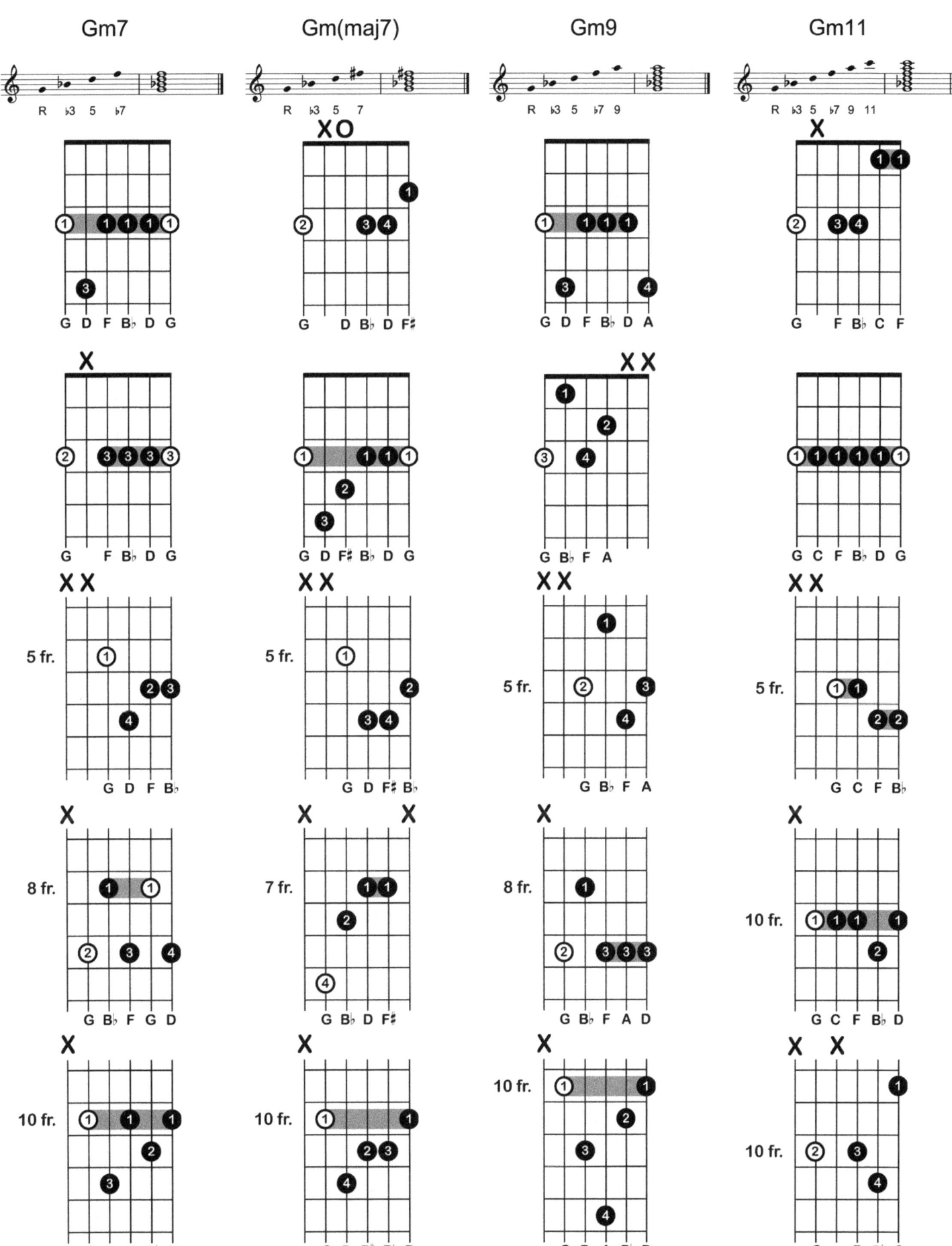

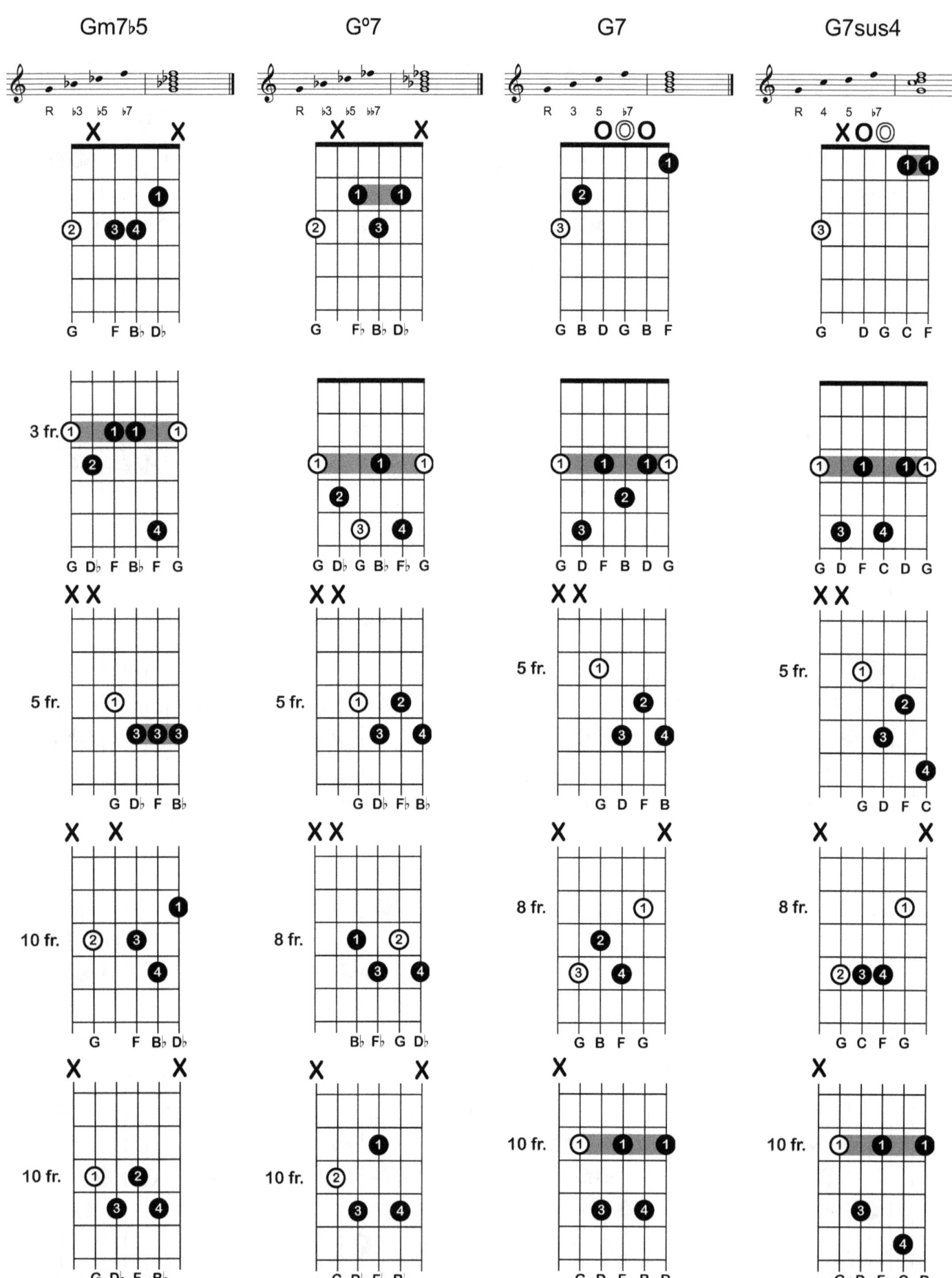

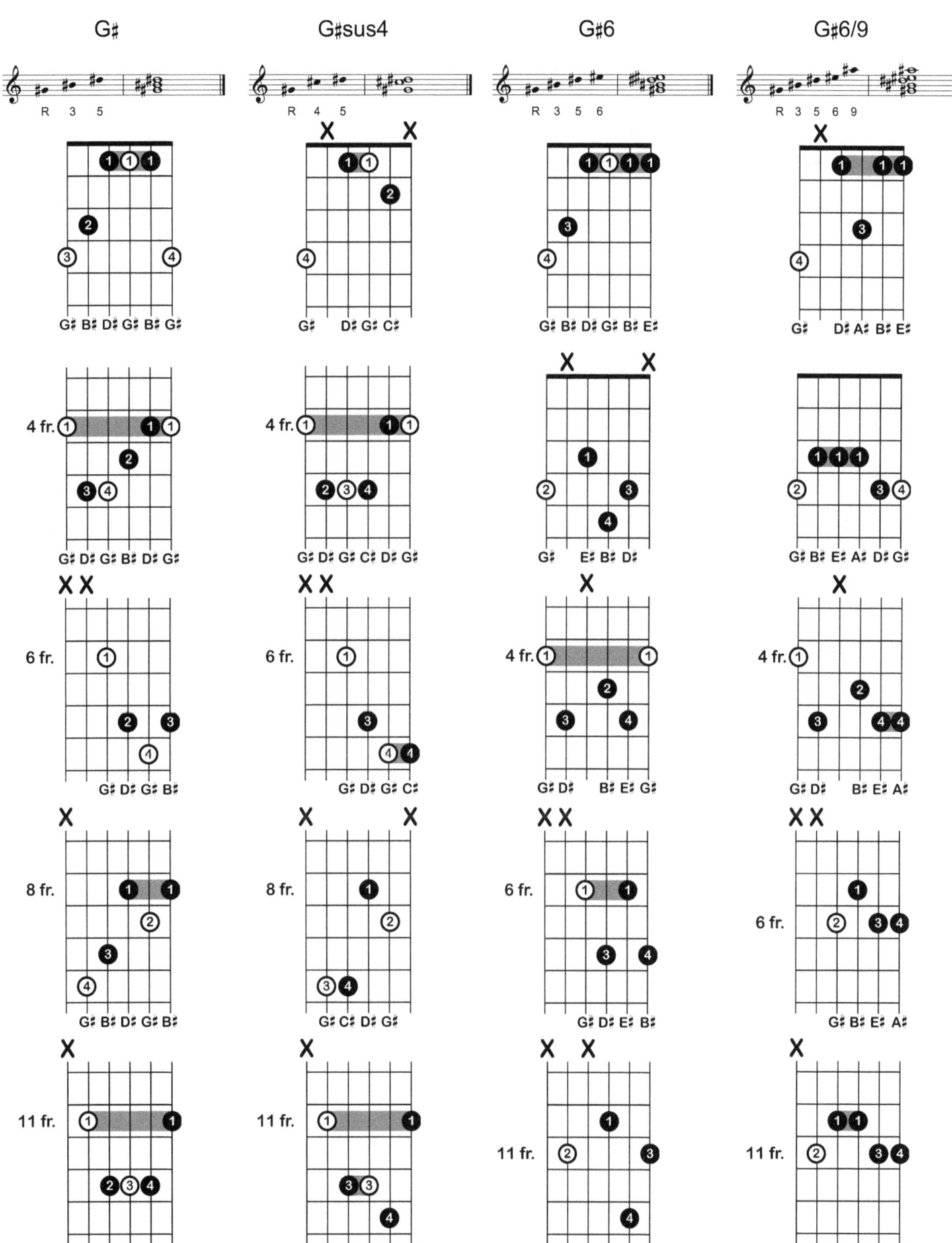

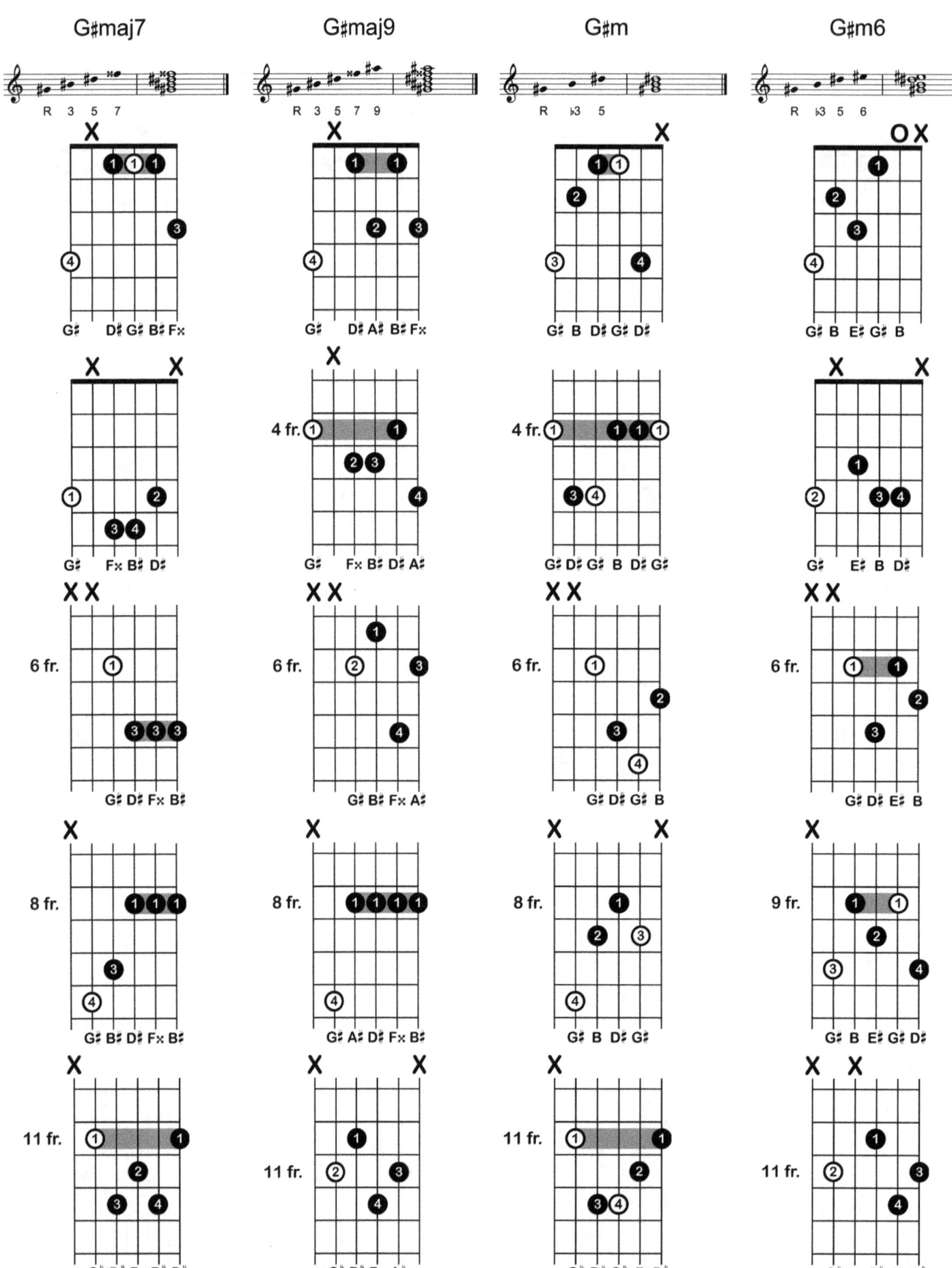

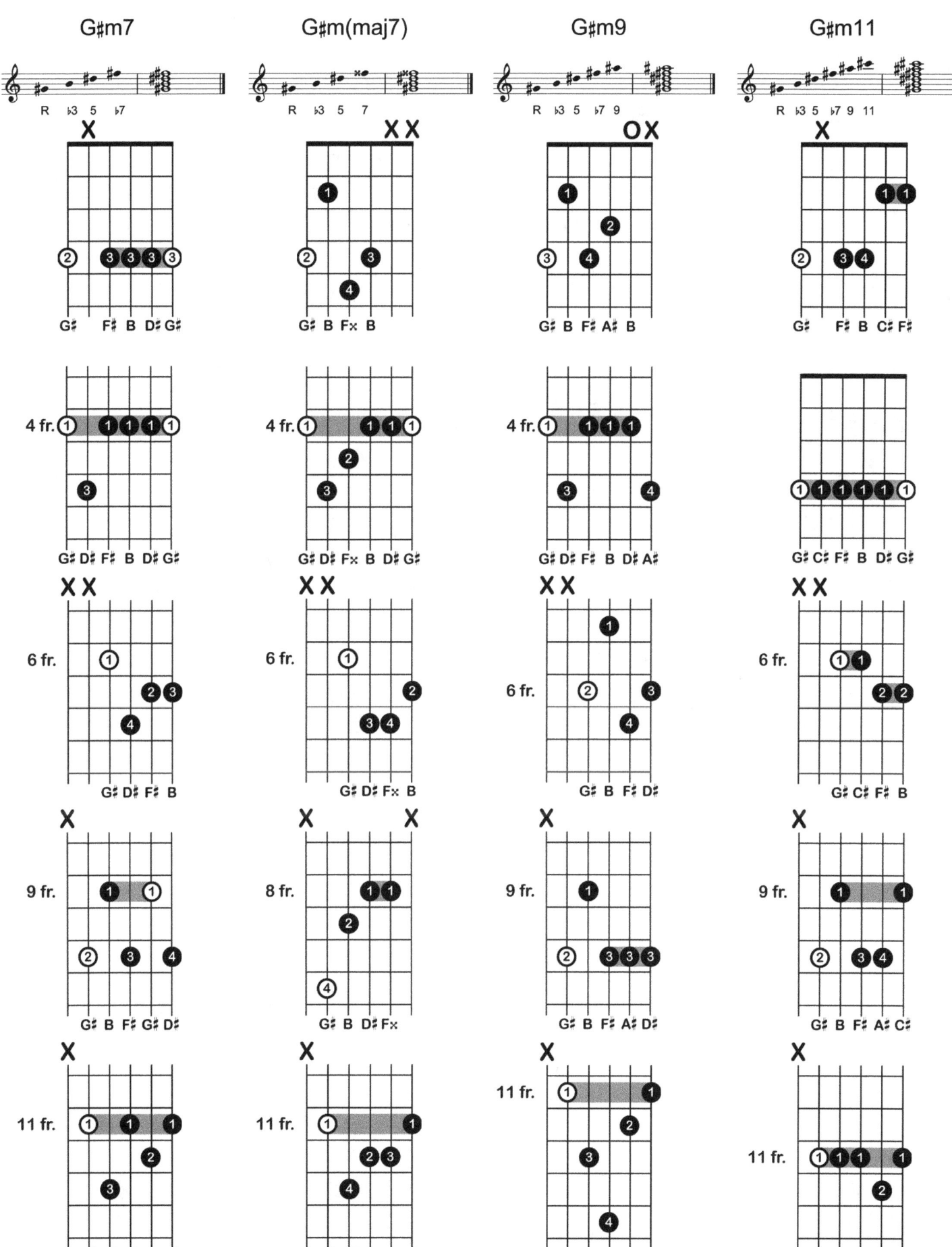

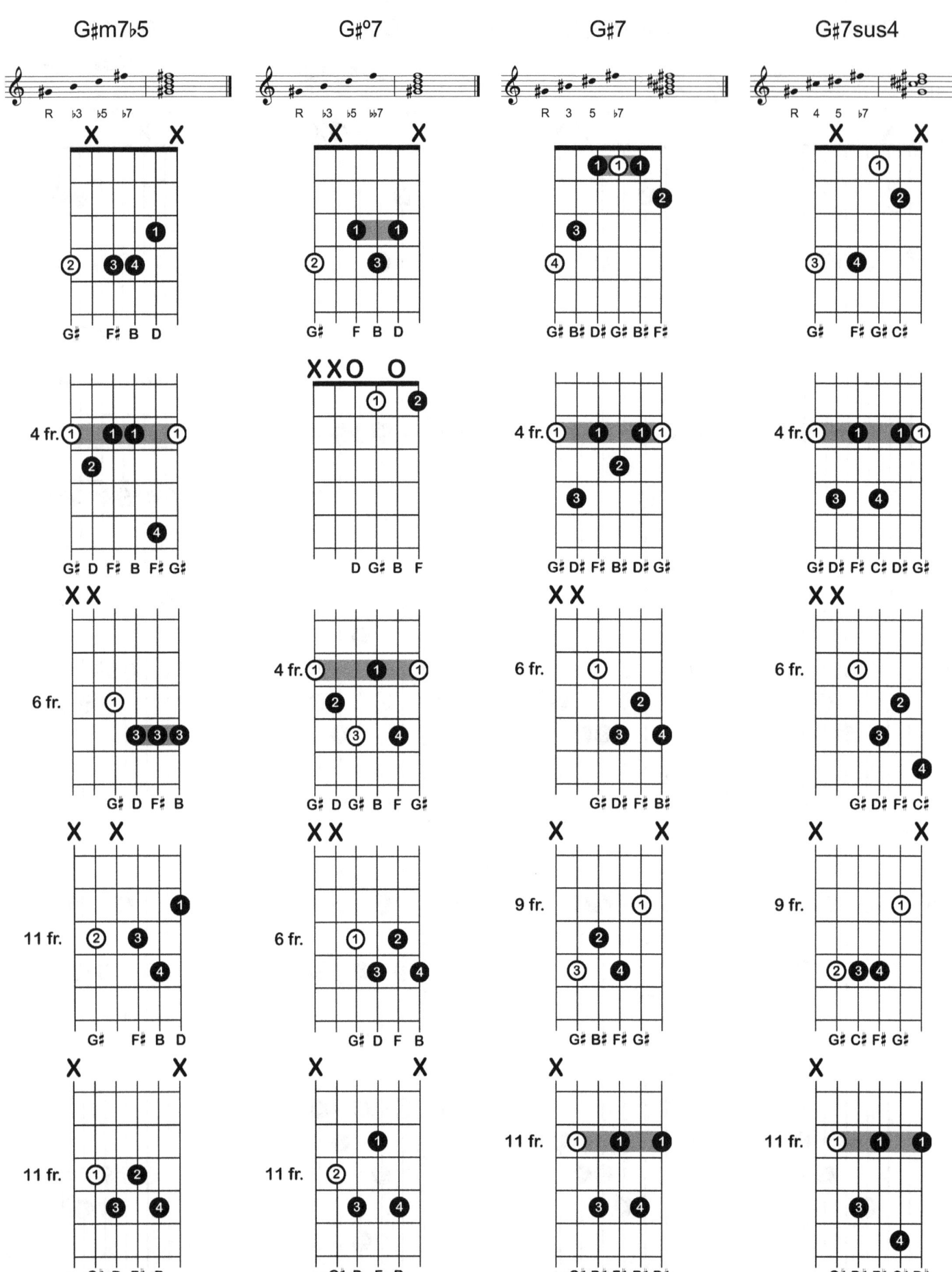

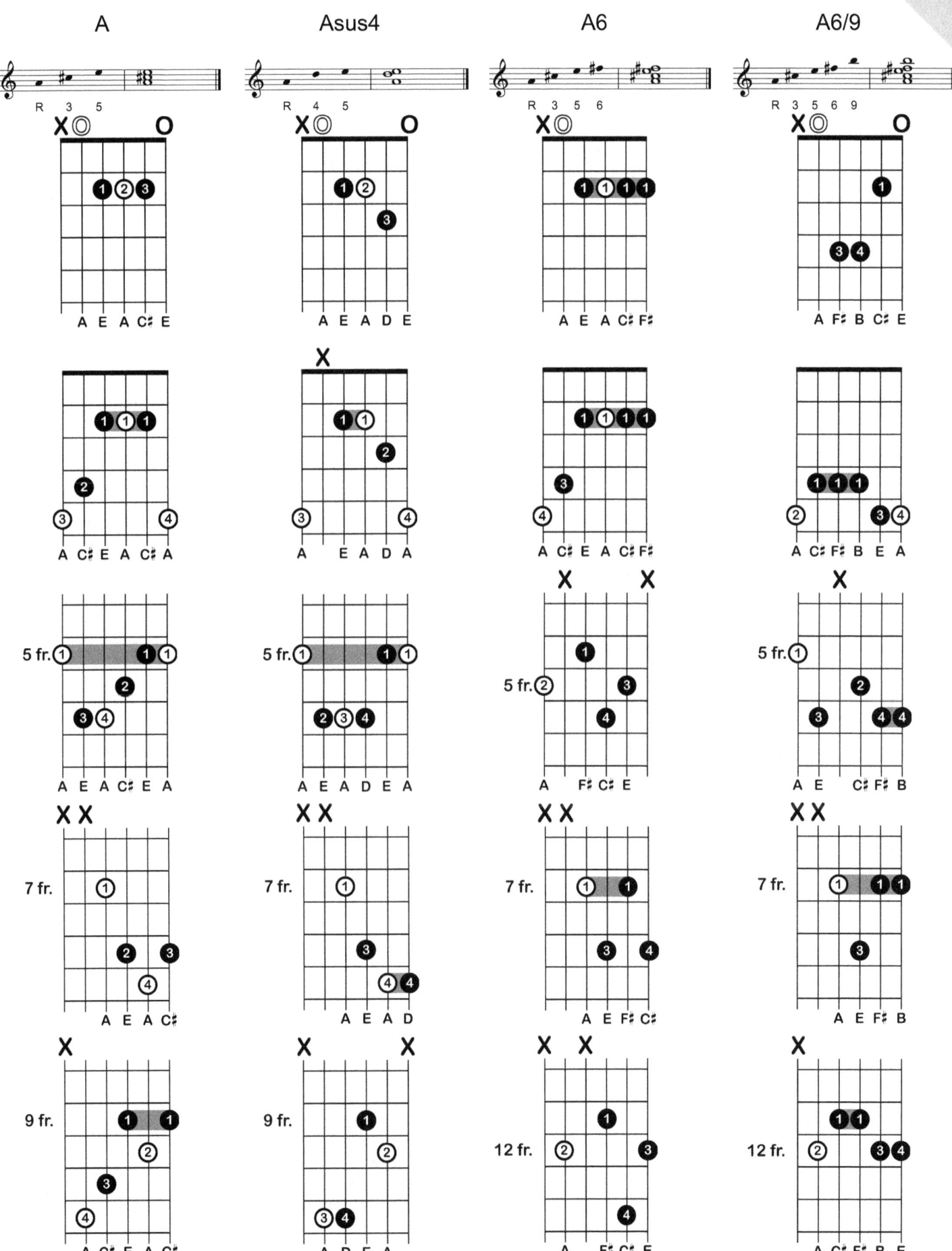

Lightning Licks Guitar Chord Bible

41

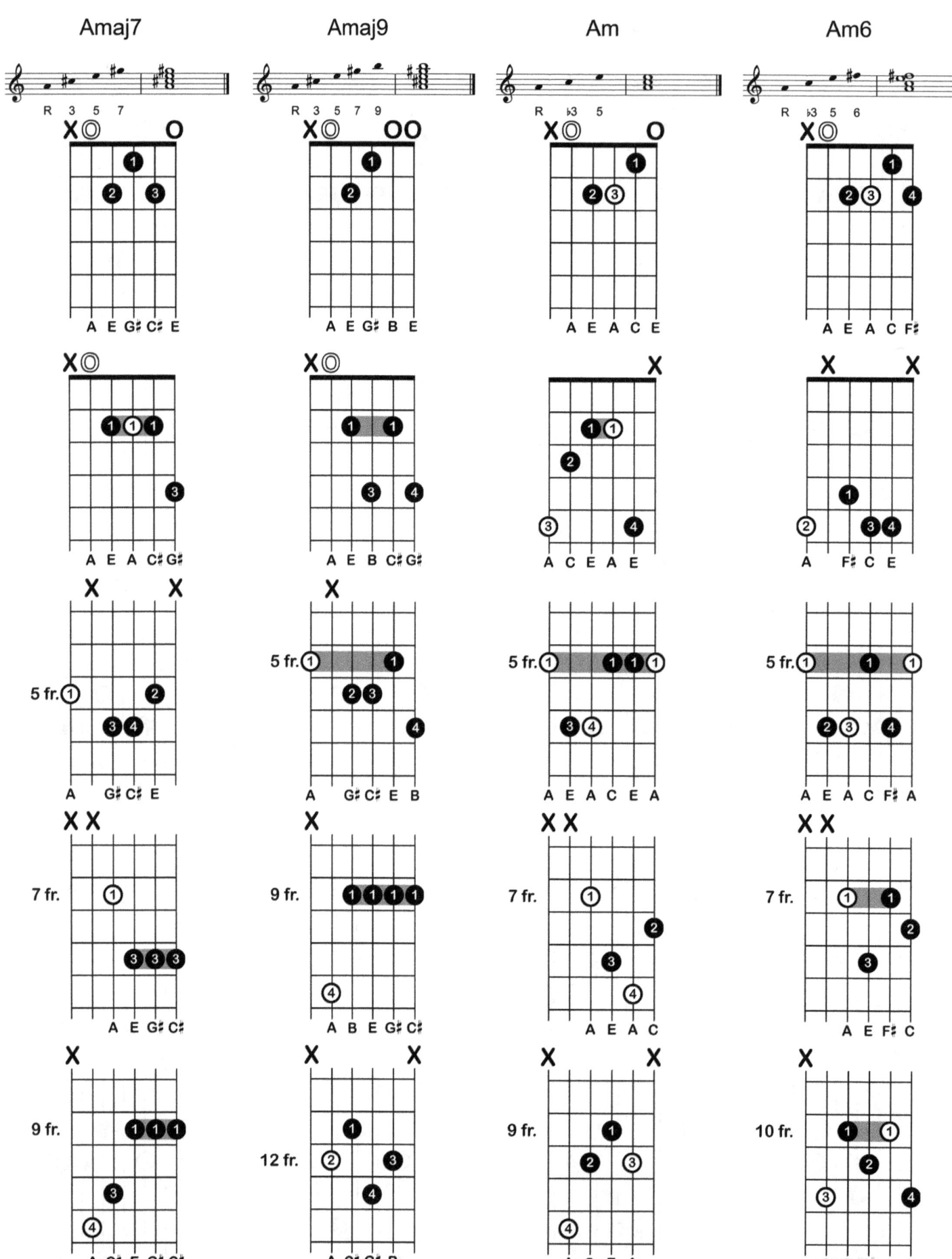

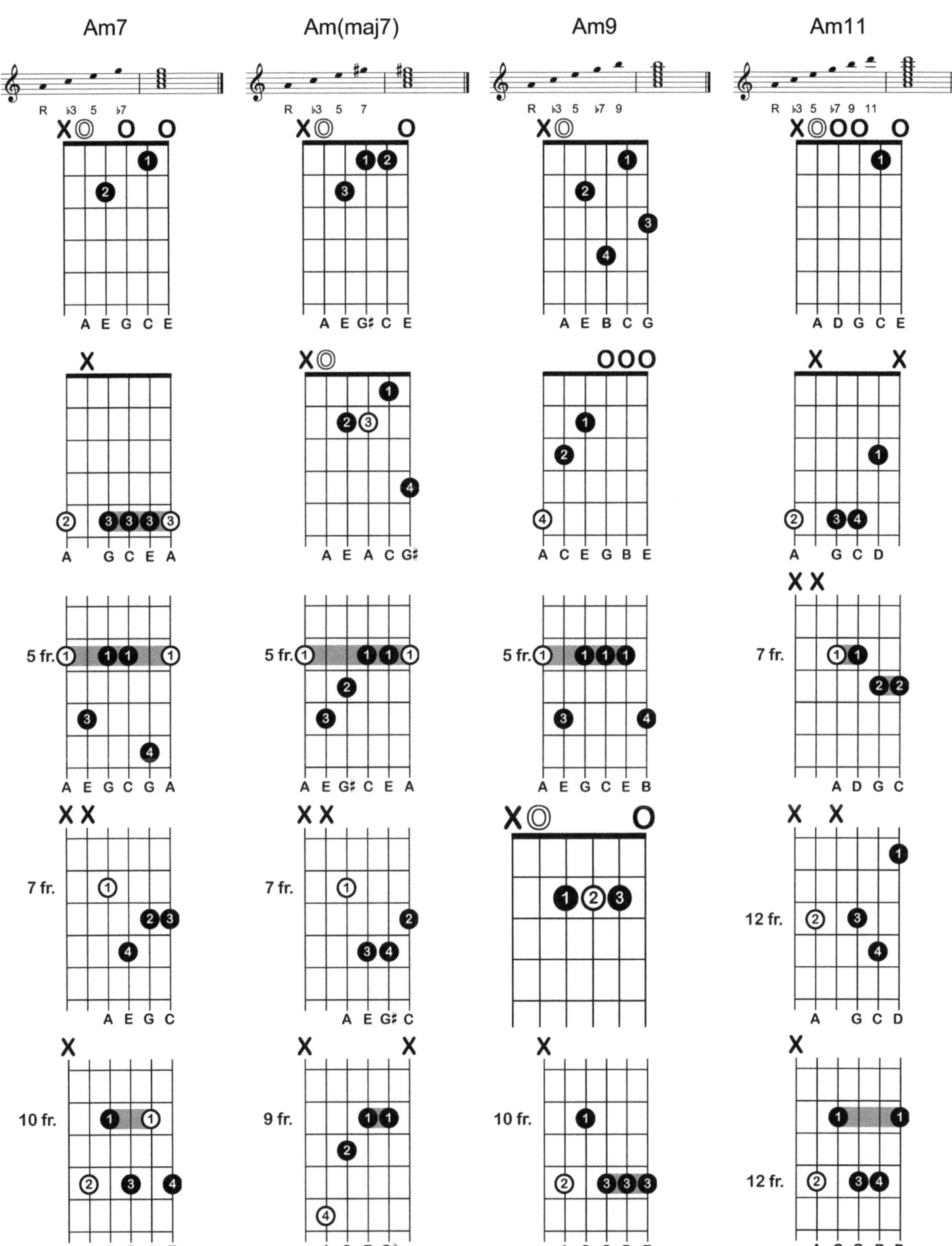

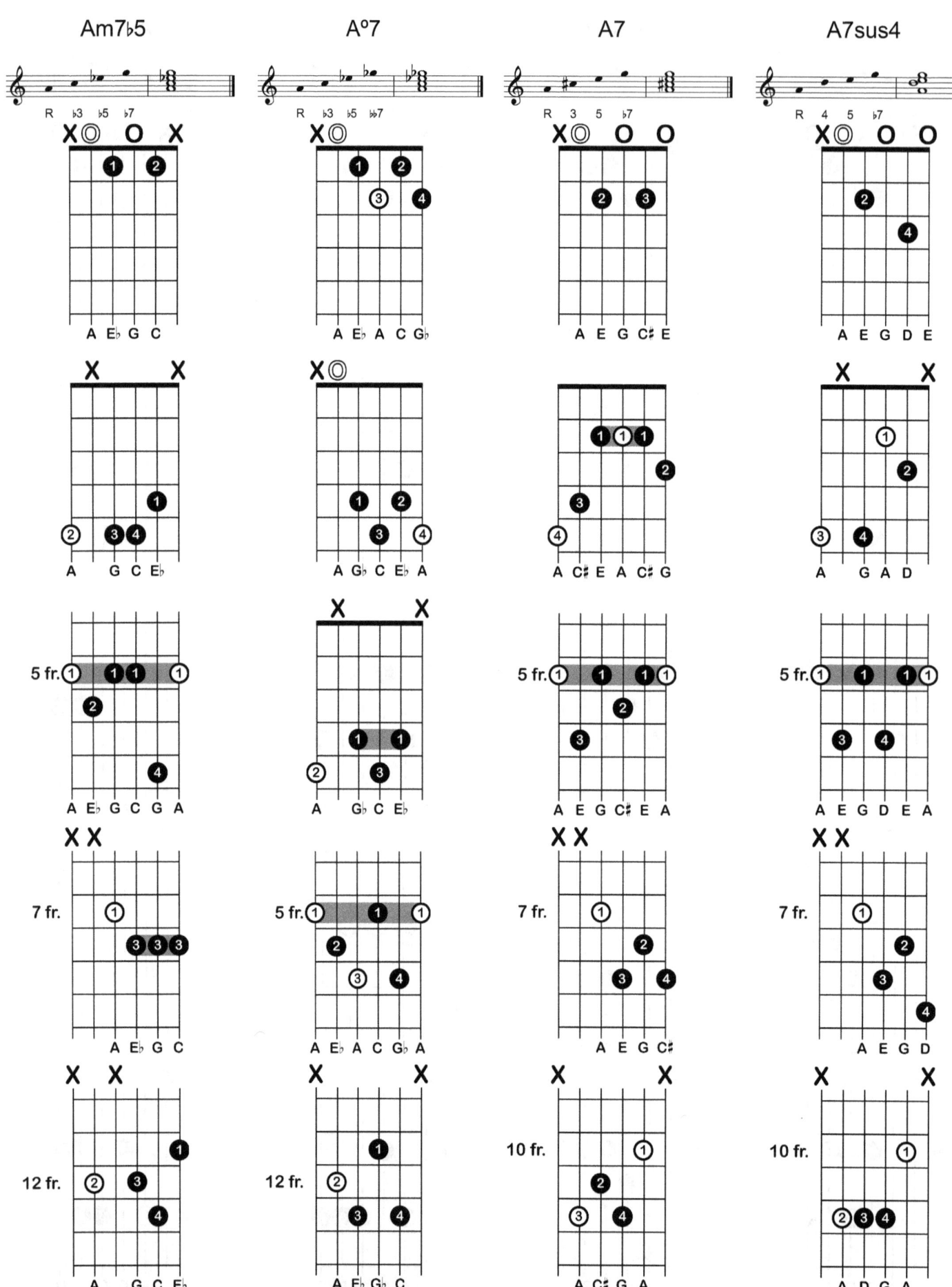

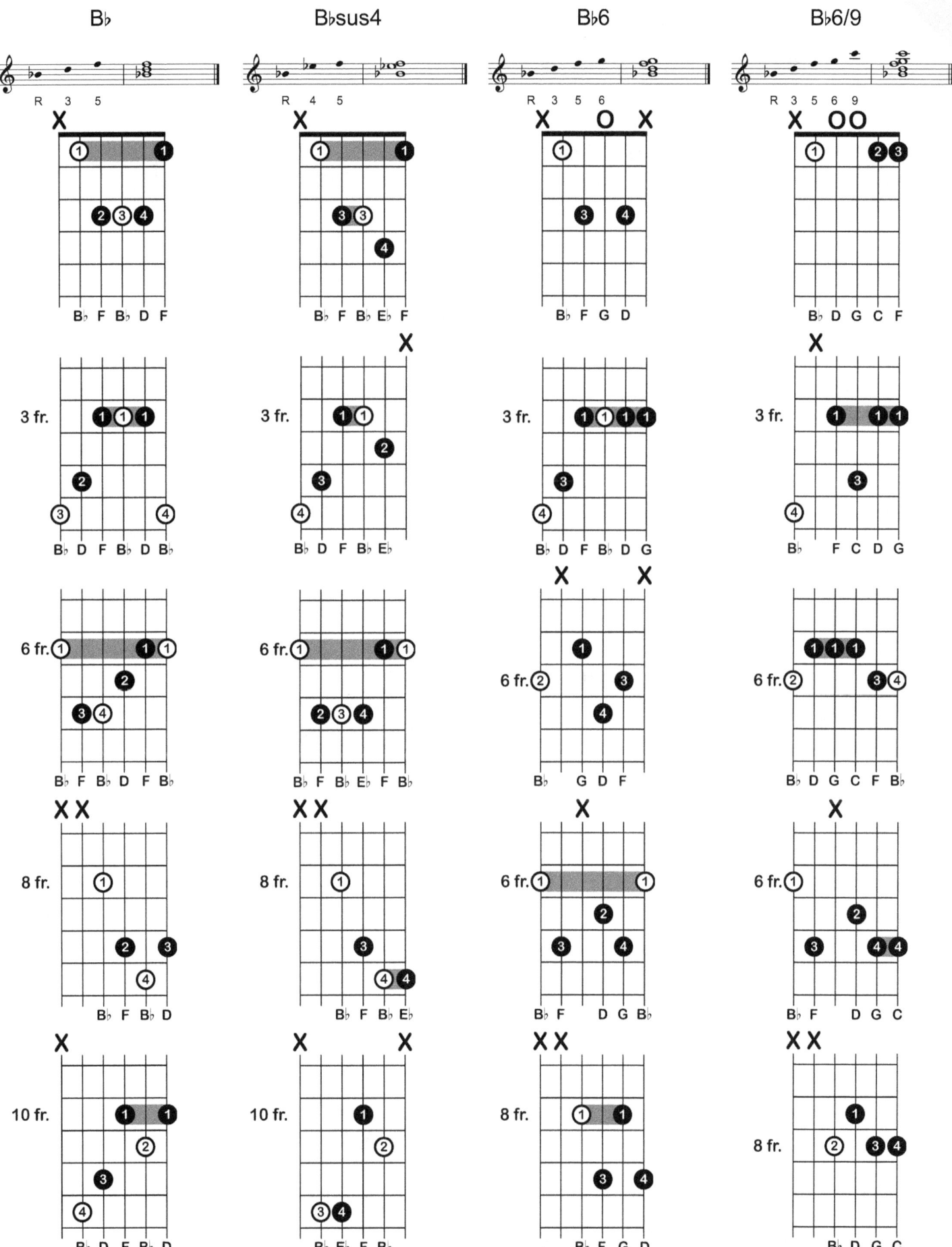

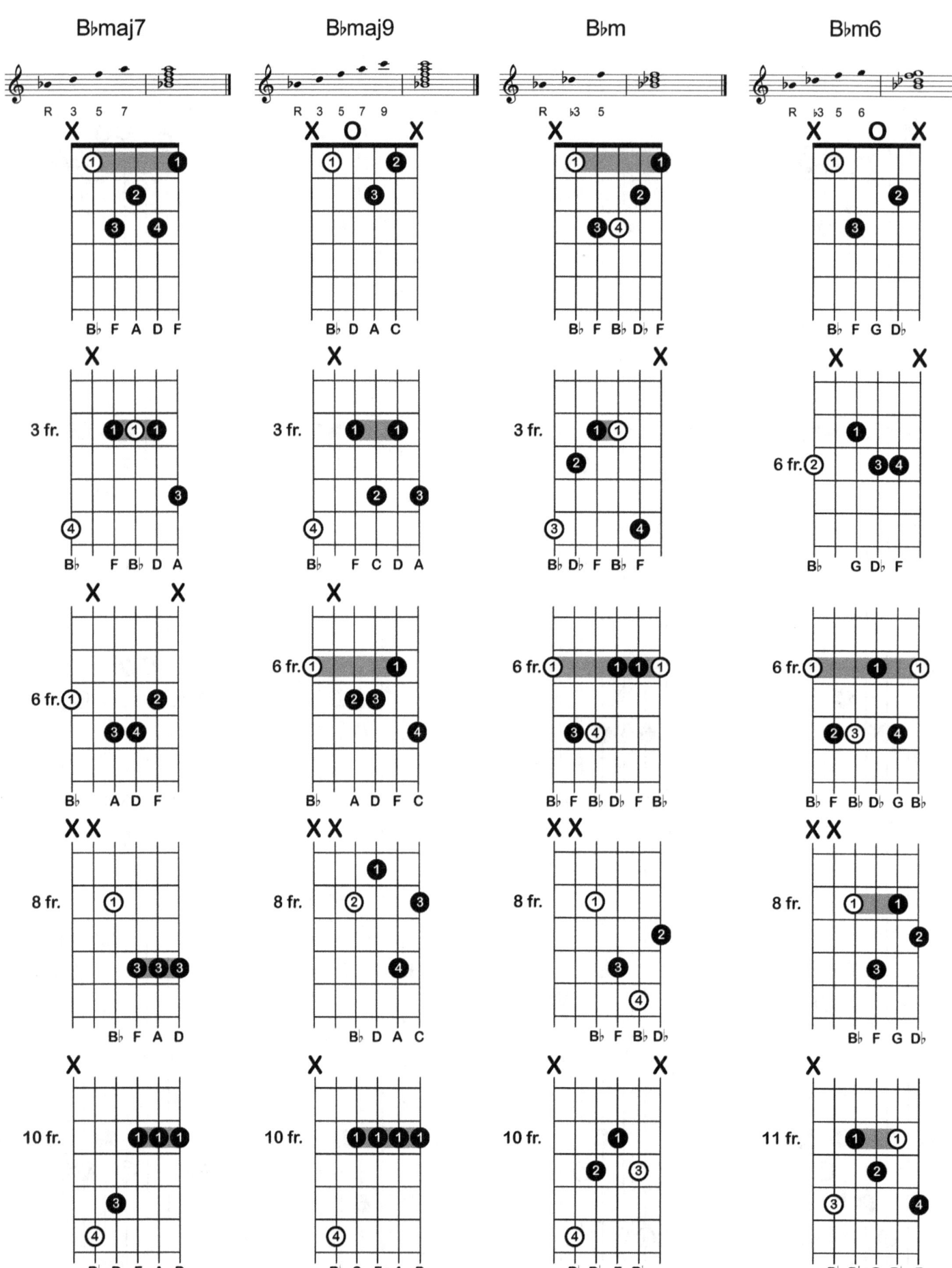

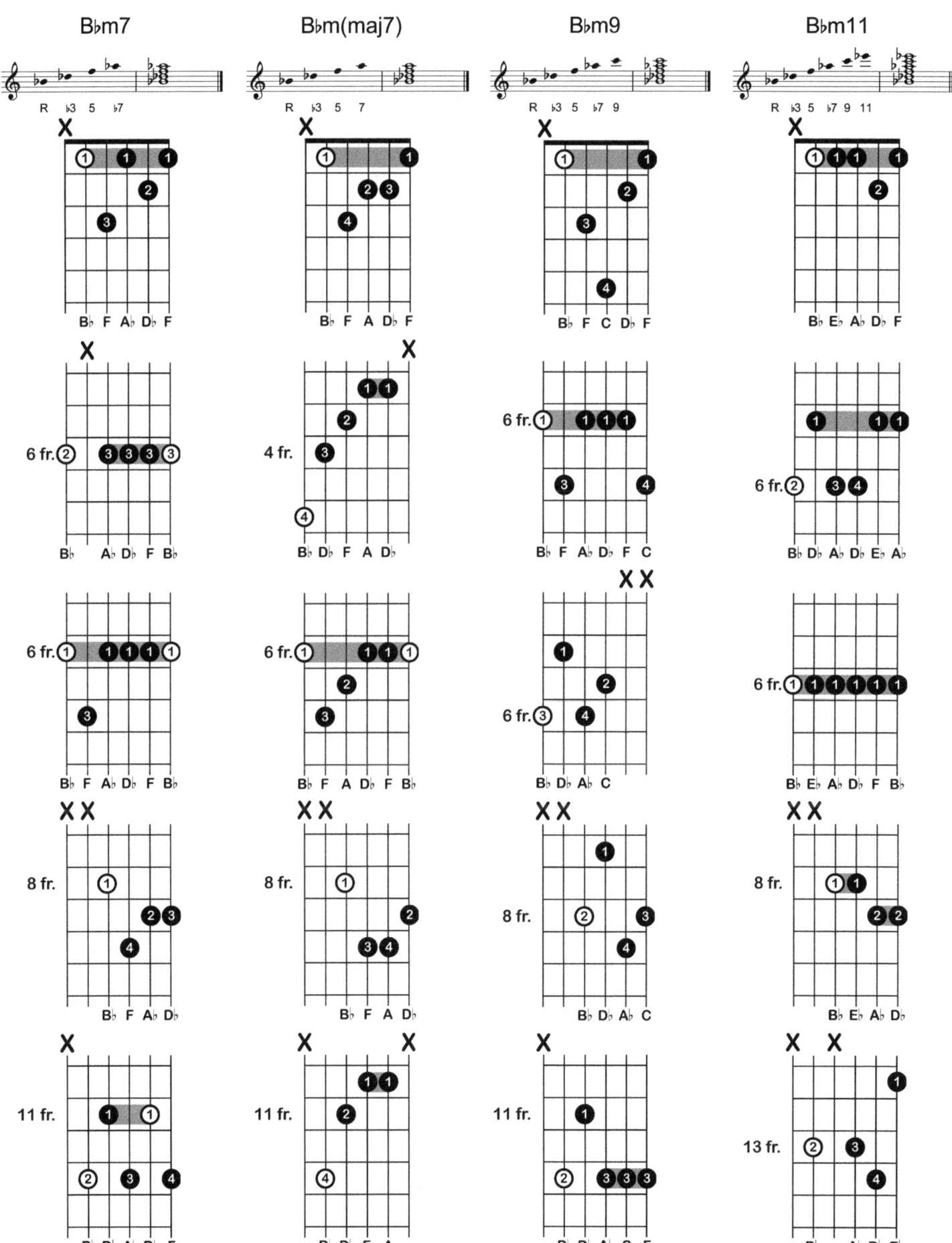

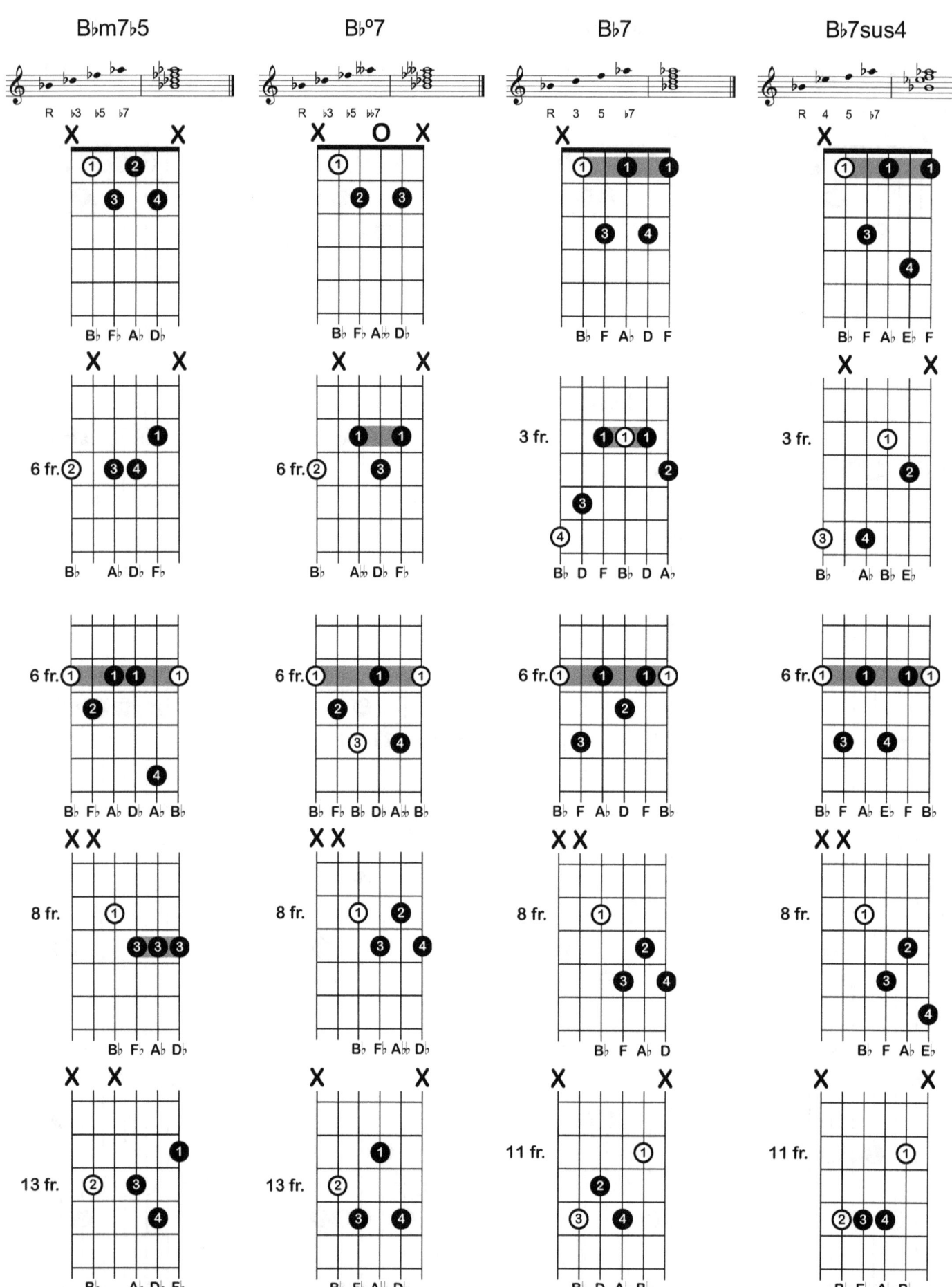

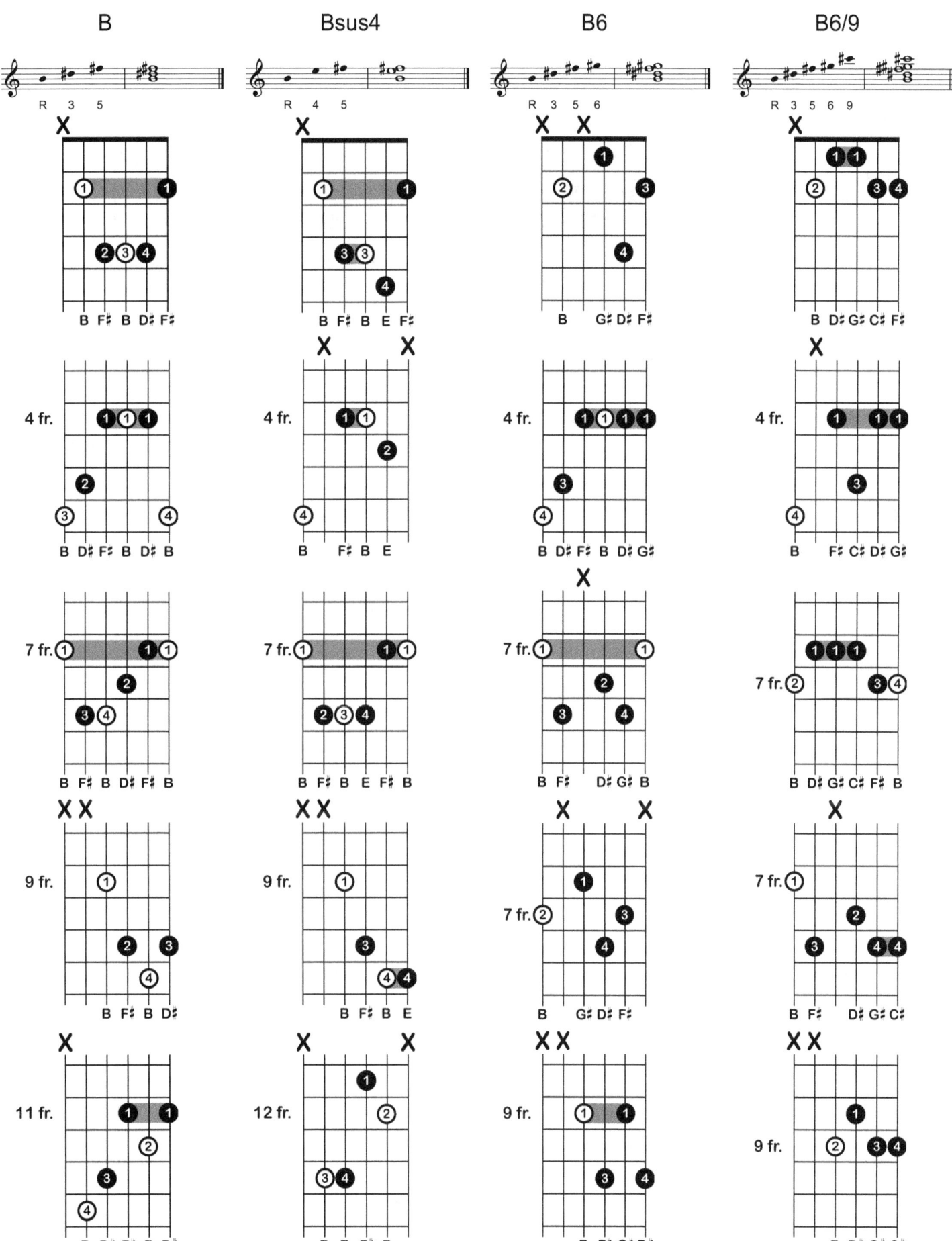

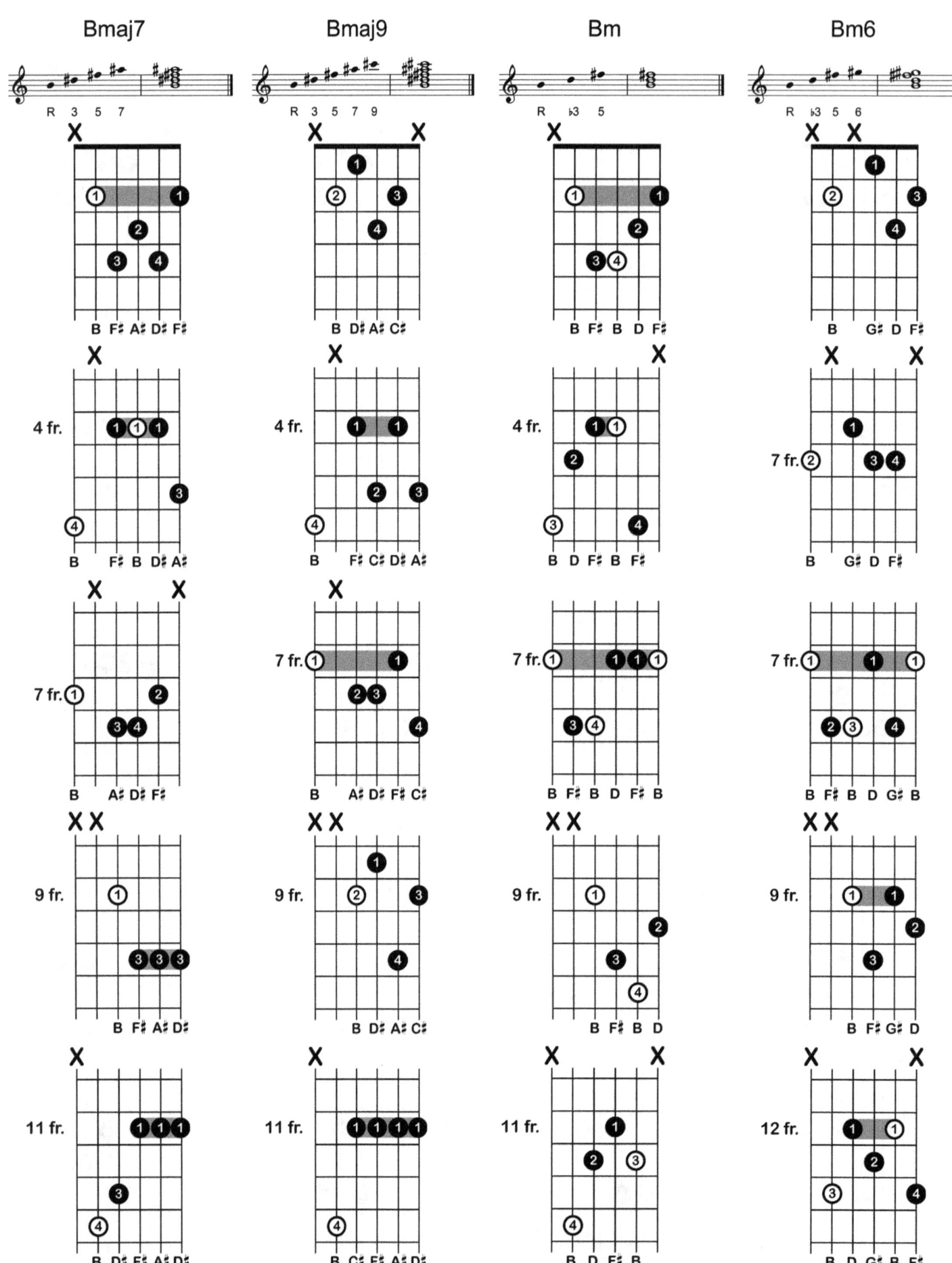

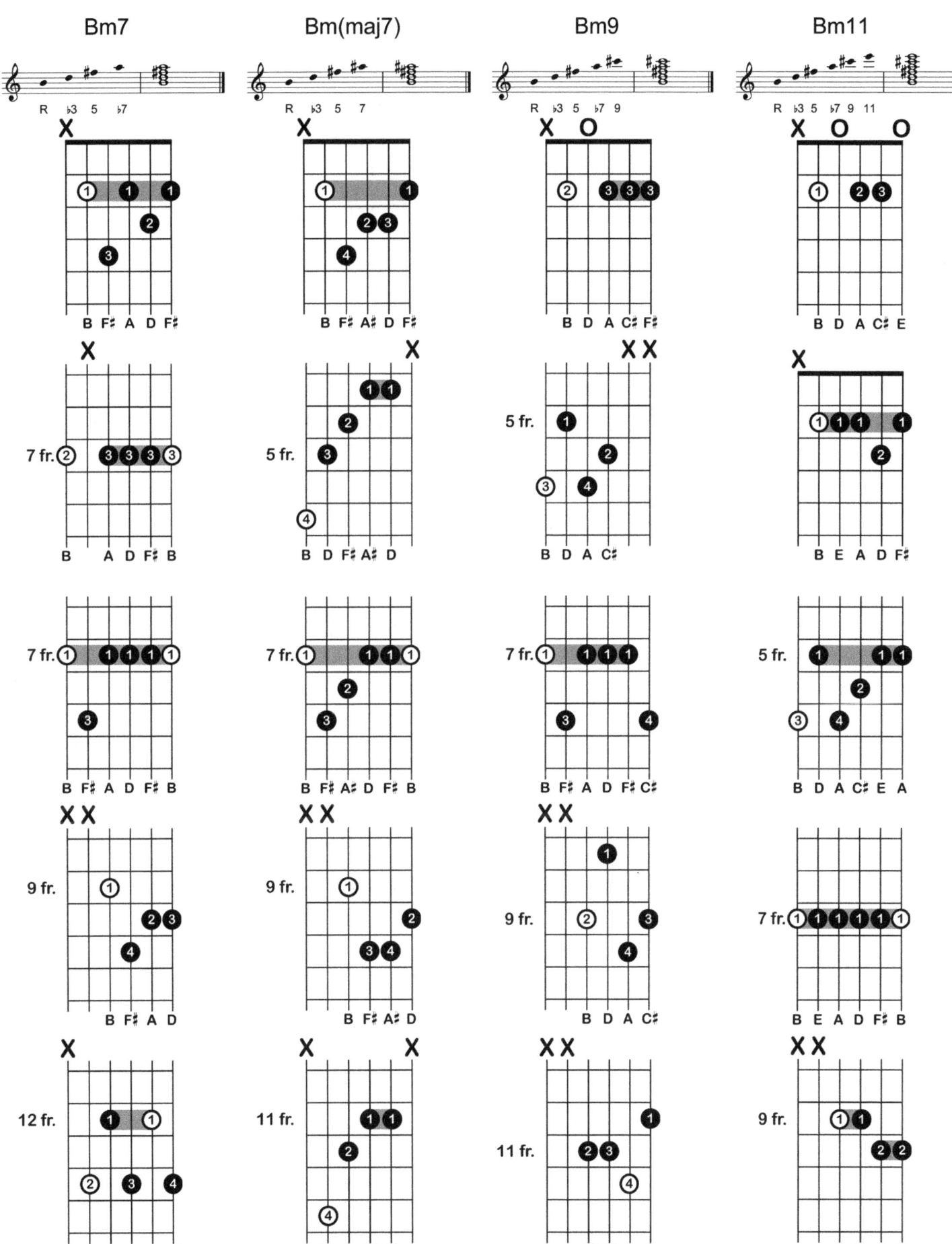

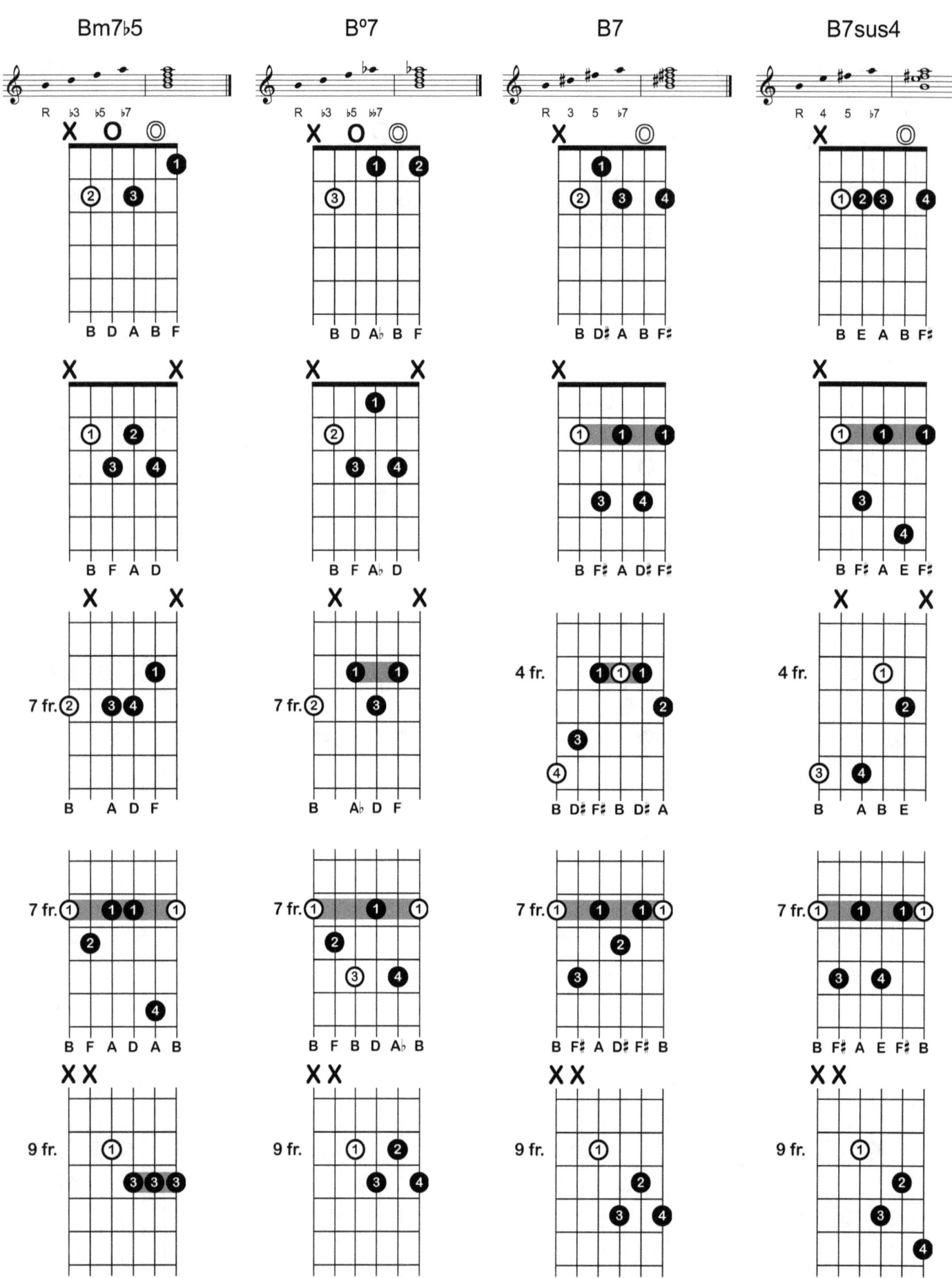

About the Author

Ed Lozano is a professional guitarist, instructor and author. He is the co-owner/music director for The Rock Underground, publisher of Guitar Teacher +, founder of Rockero Media and creator of Lightning Licks. Ed has worked with Bob Dylan, Paul Simon, Tori Amos, Stone Temple Pilots, ACDC, and many others.

As a commercial music education specialist he has produced and edited over 1,000 products and developed a curriculum of 2500+ interactive lessons. His clients include: Music Sales, Alfred, WorkshopLive, Barnes & Noble, HSN and others. In addition, Ed has ghost-written guitar methods for Keith Urban, Randy Jackson, and Esteban. He received a B.M. from Berklee College of Music.

Other Great Titles From Mayuli Press

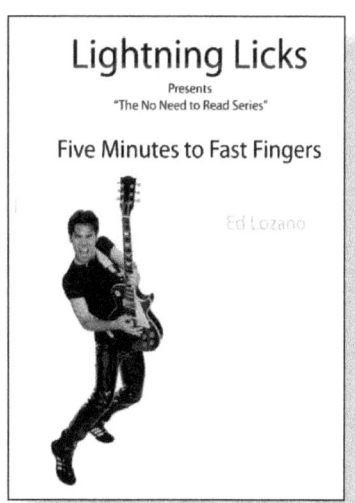